SAUSALITO PUBLIC LIBRARY

3 1111 00830 0236

S0-BPB-090

SAUSALITO PUBLIC LIBRARY

SAUSALITO PUBLIC LIBRARY

Endpapers: An engraving of the Yerebatan Sarayi – a Byzantine water cistern which provided water for Istanbul in Turkey. Thought to have been built by the emperor Constantine in the 4th century AD, the cistern was supplied with water from the aqueducts built by the Roman emperor Hadrian. A priest and three city officials anxiously examine the low water level in the cistern, while being observed by the guardian of the reservoir. The cistern still stands today.

THE ILLUSTRATED
ATLAS OF
ARCHAEOLOGY

WARWICK PRESS

Above: The Khazné, or treasury, at Petra, the capital of the Nabateans, in the mountains, north of the Red Sea. This wonderful building was carved out of solid sandstone rock by hundreds of Nabatean artisans possibly for King Aretas IV in c. AD 40. Petra was lost in the desert for many centuries, because there is only one entrance to the city, along a narrow path 2 kilometres (1½ miles) long, cut through the rock.

Left: The death mask of Tutankhamun, made of solid gold inlaid with glass and semi-precious stones. Tutankhamun became pharaoh of Egypt when he was only nine years old. He died nine years later in 1353 BC. It is probably a good likeness of the dead king. The discovery of his tomb and treasure in the Valley of the Kings in 1922 by Howard Carter was one of the most exciting episodes in the history of archaeology.

Published 1982 by Warwick Press,
730 Fifth Avenue, New York, New York 10019.

First published in Great Britain by
Longman Group Limited 1982.

Copyright © 1982 by Grisewood & Dempsey Ltd.

Printed in Italy by Vallardi Industrie Grafiche.

Library of Congress Catalog Card No. 81-71549

ISBN 0-531-09207-0

Contents

Author

Sue Rollin, M.A.

Editor

Adrian Sington

Illustrations

Jillian Burgess Artists

Maps by

Malcolm Porter

Above: Taking the impression of a Mesopotamian cylinder seal. Every well-to-do citizen had his own seal. They were rolled into wet clay used to seal merchandise or used to sign a contract, leaving the impression of the design behind. They were generally finely engraved with religious scenes.

Left: Inca Indians walking down a street in Cuzco, the ancient capital of the Inca empire. The Incas were great engineers; notice the huge blocks of stone, fitted closely together, without mortar, used in building this wall. Today it is the Inca walls that stand up to the frequent earthquakes, when more modern buildings collapse.

Engraving of the Grave Circle inside the city walls of Mycenae after excavations by Schliemann. Schliemann dug inside the circle of stones and revealed the famous shaft-graves sunk into the ground. There were many rich treasures in these graves – gold and silver vases, jewellery, swords of gold, silver, copper and bronze and gold death masks. Schliemann thought he had found the tombs of Agamemnon and Clytemnestra, king and queen of Mycenae at the time of the Trojan War. However, we now know that all the graves belong to an earlier period.

Story of Archaeology

Archaeology is the study of the remains of human life long ago. Archaeologists discover and record ancient objects such as tools and weapons and the remains of buildings and monuments such as houses, temples and tombs. From these they build up a picture of how people lived in the past. Many archaeological remains are buried in the ground, and archaeologists must uncover these by *excavation*, that is by digging in the earth.

There are two main kinds of archaeology. One is the archaeology that deals with human history before writing was invented, called *prehistoric* archaeology. The other deals with the remains of people who had written documents, called *historic* archaeology. Writing began in the Near East about 5500 years ago, and slowly spread to other parts of the world.

The Origins of Archaeology
From the 16th century onwards European scholars became interested in the ancient civilizations of Greece and Rome. Many people visited ancient ruins and collected old and rare objects. During the 18th century there were early excavations in Italy, at Roman sites such as Pompeii and Herculaneum which were buried under ash and lava when the volcano Vesuvius erupted in AD 79.

In the 18th century, people also began to study the ancient sites of northern Europe. William Stukeley was a famous British archaeologist who travelled around Britain making drawings and descriptions of many places, including Stonehenge. Collectors and travellers were also interested in Ancient Egypt and the Near East. When Napoleon Bonaparte led a military expedition to Egypt in 1798, for example, he took with him many scholars to study Egyptian geography and ancient monuments.

As more and more ancient objects were found, it became necessary to *classify* them, that is to arrange them in different groups. C. J. Thomsen, who worked for the Danish National Museum, founded in 1816, arranged the museum's antiquities according to what they were made of: stone, bronze and iron. He realized that these three groups represented three different periods of time.

Stone was the earliest of these. Since then archaeologists have described these periods as the *Stone Age*, the *Bronze Age* and the *Iron Age*. Later an Englishman, John Lubbock, divided the Stone Age into two periods. Most tools of the *Palaeolithic* or Old Stone Age period were made by chipping away fragments of stone to get a particular shape. These are called *flaked* stone tools. In the *Neolithic* or New Stone Age there were many *polished* stone tools, especially axes. Grouping objects in this way according to their form is called *typology*.

The Antiquity of Man

Until the 19th century most people believed in the biblical account of the creation of the world, which they thought happened in 4004 BC. In the 19th century, however, scientists made discoveries which showed that the world and humans were very much older than that. The most famous of these scientists was Charles Darwin. His theory was that the plants and animals of his day had not been created suddenly but had developed slowly over a very long time from earlier, much simpler forms. He published this theory of *evolution* in 1859. *Fossils*, which are the remains of long dead plants and animals preserved in rocks, are very important for the study of evolution. Among the fossils found in different parts of the world are the remains of earlier types of human.

Early Civilizations

During the 19th and early 20th centuries archaeologists uncovered the remains of early civilizations in many parts of the world. In Egypt the most spectacular discovery was the tomb of Tutankhamun in 1922. Through excavations in the Near East the treasures of ancient Sumer, Babylonia, Assyria and Persia were found and the ancient languages were deciphered.

The German businessman, Heinrich Schliemann, who had always been fascinated by the legends of the Trojan Wars and the ancient Greek heroes, discovered and excavated the ancient city of Troy in 1870. He later dug at Mycenae and other sites in Greece. In Crete the Englishman, Sir Arthur Evans, discovered the remains of an unknown civilization, in 1899, which he called Minoan. Another lost civilization was found by British archaeologists in India. It was named the Indus civilization. Expeditions to China, Africa and the Americas also produced remarkable finds. By the Second World War there was enough information to write a history of the ancient world.

Since the Second World War archaeology has changed in many ways. Archaeologists now want to construct a fuller picture of human history and its development by studying such things as the distribution of settlements and what connections they had with each other, how these societies were

organized and the ancient *environment* or surroundings of archaeological sites. Such studies are made possible by archaeologists working together with other scholars and scientists. By using modern scientific methods, sites can now be excavated more accurately and the finds can be examined in more detail. New discoveries and new ideas mean that our picture of the past is constantly changing and will continue to do so in the future.

Left: The most famous discovery of Napoleon's expedition to Egypt was the Rosetta Stone, which provided the key to the decipherment of Ancient Egyptian. The inscriptions on the surface of the stone are in Greek, a language which could already be read, and also in Demotic and hieroglyphic – the two scripts used to write the language of ancient Egypt. Using the Greek inscription to help him, a Frenchman, J. F. Champollion, deciphered the ancient hieroglyphic script in 1822, after working on it, for 14 years, since the age of 18.

Below: Ancient Sumerian jewellery from Ur in southern Iraq. Some of the most spectacular treasures of ancient Sumer come from Ur, which was excavated from 1922–1934 by the English archaeologist Sir Leonard Woolley. Near a later temple a huge cemetery of nearly 2000 graves was discovered. Seventeen of these were Royal Tombs, with very rich contents. In one of them, known as the 'Great Death Pit', 74 bodies were found. Possibly these were attendants who had been sacrificed when their master died so that they could serve him in the afterlife. Most of the bodies were of women, adorned with jewellery of gold, silver and semi-precious stones.

In the Field

The first problem which faces archaeologists is the choice of a site to dig. Because there is limited time and money for archaeology it is only possible to excavate some of the many archaeological sites. Many sites are chosen because they are about to be destroyed by modern industrial development, such as road construction or the building of factories or offices. This is called *rescue archaeology*. Archaeologists choose other sites for excavation because they think they will produce information which will fill particular gaps in our knowledge of the past.

Locating the Site

The remains of many sites are visible above ground. These are often marked on maps, such as the Ordnance Survey maps in Britain. New sites are discovered in several ways. One of the best methods is to walk over a chosen area, looking for archaeological finds and features. Often things like broken pottery and coins appear on the surface of a ploughed field, for example, when no remains of buildings or other features can be seen. This way of finding and mapping archaeological sites is called *ground survey* or *field-walking*. More details about archaeological features, especially those which are buried beneath the ground, can be obtained by using modern *geophysical survey* methods. One of these methods is called *electrical resistivity*. The resistance of the ground to an electric current passed

through it changes when the current meets buried features such as walls or ditches. These changes can be recorded using special instruments. A similar method is known as *magnetometry*. The magnetic field of the ground also varies where there are archaeological remains below the surface, and scientific instruments can record the variations. Archaeologists can use the results of these survey methods to make a plan of some of the buried archaeological features before they begin to dig.

Another important method of locating and planning archaeological sites is *aerial photography*. From the air the plan of a site and its surrounding area can often be very clearly seen. Sometimes from the air things are visible which cannot be seen from the ground, especially when the sun is low on the horizon and casts deep shadows. Buried

Finds assistants sorting out pottery and other finds from the Mycenean site of Tiryns, Greece. After everything has been sorted out, it is labelled and packed away in boxes, like those seen in the background here. Then it is transported to a museum or archaeological institute for further study after the end of the excavation.

An aerial photograph taken with an infra-red camera, showing rectangular and round structures buried beneath the ground. Infra-red light is invisible to human beings. It is the form in which heat is radiated. It can be detected by special photographic films. Unlike an ordinary aerial photograph, an infra-red photograph does not pick up shadows or crop marks, but small and different amounts of radiated heat. Crops growing at different rates or under slightly different conditions give off different amounts of heat. Buried archaeological features, which affect crop growth, therefore often show up on an infra-red photograph. Several archaeological sites have been discovered using this method.

features can affect the way in which crops grow in the fields. When there are brick or stone remains below the ground, the crop will not grow as well as elsewhere, and when there are buried ditches or pits the crop grows better because there is more moisture there than in the rest of the field. These *crop marks* often show up very well on aerial photographs.

Excavation

Although different types of site require different methods of digging, certain basic methods are common to most excavations. If there is nothing visible above the ground, a number of trenches are dug in different parts of the site to find out its approximate size and the depth and date of the archaeological remains. After this the top soil can be stripped away from a large area to expose the uppermost archaeological layer. Modern earth-moving machinery is often used for this. An archaeological site consists of different layers of material which represent the remains of human occupation over a period of time. These layers make up the *stratigraphy* of a site. The archaeologists and their helpers carefully remove the layers one after the other. The main tool used for this is a builder's pointing trowel. Most things are found during trowelling, but by sieving the earth afterwards it is possible to recover any small finds that have been overlooked.

Recording and cataloguing

It is important to keep a record of everything found on an archaeological site. Every layer of material should be described. The position and depth of all objects must be noted. Drawings and photographs are made of all features such as house foundations, hearths and pits. So that all finds and features can be recorded accurately, the site is divided up into a network of squares, called a *grid*. Each square is given a number and the exact position of everything within it is measured and marked on a plan. A special instrument known as a *dumpy level* is often used to measure the exact height above sea level of the different parts of the site and the things discovered there.

When excavation of a particular area has been completed, detailed drawings are made of the sides of the trench. These are called *section drawings* and they show the stratigraphy of the site. Sections are also often cut through important features before they are completely excavated, and these sections are also drawn. All objects found during excavation are given a number and catalogued in a finds book. Where possible the finds are washed and cleaned on the site and the number is written on them in ink. The people who do this work are called *finds assistants*. They then sort out the finds into types and according to which level they come from and pack them away in plastic bags for further study after the end of the excavation.

Above: Excavating Roman remains in Frankfurt, Germany. The archaeologist is measuring the height of the wall and the position of the different stones so that she can make an accurate drawing on the plan in front of her.

Left: A schoolboy unearthing a skeleton from an ancient tomb near Budapest in Hungary.

11

Science & Archaeology

Compared to ten years ago, the amount of additional information which can be deduced from archaeological evidence using scientific techniques is enormous, and is increasing every year. Most sites contain a lot of biological evidence which can produce information about such things as the climate, animals and plants of a particular period. Such evidence includes the bones of animals, birds and fishes, and the remains of vegetation such as seeds and pollen grains. Scientists can usually tell whether bones come from wild animals or farm animals. This is because the bones of a domesticated species of wild animal gradually change shape over a period of generations. For instance, analysis of human bones can tell us about common diseases.

Materials like leather, textiles and wood are often not well preserved on archaeological sites. However, under very wet or very dry conditions such objects can be recovered in a good state of preservation.

The perfect condition of the human bodies found in the peat-bogs of Denmark is a good example of preservation in waterlogged ground. Many of these bodies, such as the famous Tollund man, still had their skin, hair and clothing. Such finds must be kept under water until they reach a museum laboratory, where they are slowly dried and the water replaced by oil or carbowax. A dry climate, such as in Egypt, can also produce well-preserved objects, and these must also be chemically treated so that they do not decay.

The cleaning, treatment and restoration of archaeological finds by museum scientists and technicians is called *conservation*. Many excavated objects need conservation. For example, metals such as bronze and iron are often heavily rusted when they come out of the earth. Most pottery and glass vessels are broken but can be reconstructed if many or all of the pieces have been found. After conservation metals, pottery and glass can be studied under a powerful microscope or analysed by a technique known as *spectroscopy* to find out exactly what chemical elements they are composed of. Such techniques give us important information on methods of manufacture and also on trade, especially if the original source of the material used to make the objects can be found – this is often difficult.

View of the particle accelerator at the radiocarbon laboratory in Oxford. Particle accelerators are only just starting to be used for radiocarbon dating. A sample of material to be dated is specially prepared and accelerated through large electric and magnetic fields. The Carbon 14 atoms separate from the other atoms and can be collected and measured. One of the great advantages of this method is that only very small samples of materials are needed.

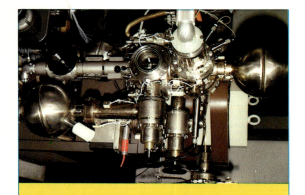

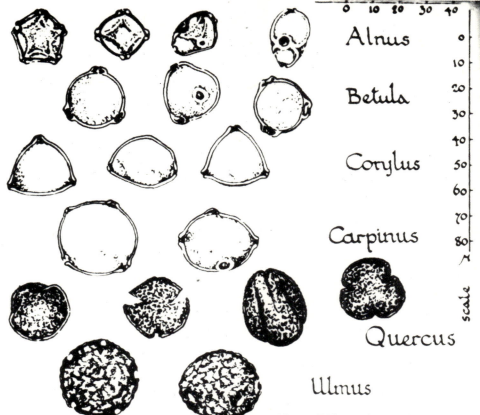

Dating methods

One of the most important modern scientific advances has been the development of dating techniques. The most famous of these is *radio-carbon* dating. On the death of any living thing, whether animal or vegetable, the amount of the substance known as *Carbon 14* – which all living organisms contain – gradually decays. The rate of decay is the same at all times and in all conditions. Every living thing has only a very small amount of Carbon 14 within it. Large plants or animals have more Carbon 14 in them than small ones, but the percentage of Carbon 14 to their bulk is always the same. About 5730 years after death, there will be exactly half the original amount of Carbon 14 left. By measuring the percentage of Carbon 14 which is left in bones or wood, charcoal or other plant remains from archaeological sites, the date of death can be calculated.

Radio-carbon dating is used for remains up to about 50,000 years old. For older remains a similar method, called *potassium-argon* dating, can sometimes be used. The mass spectrometer is used in this type of dating.

Another important dating method is called *thermoluminescence*. It is used for dating pottery and glass. These are heated until an amount of energy in the form of light is released. The greater the age of the pot, the greater the thermoluminescence, that is, the amount of light.

Other scientific dating methods include *obsidian hydration* dating. Obsidian is a volcanic glass which was used to make tools in many of the areas of the world where it occurs. These tools can be dated because obsidian absorbs water from its surroundings at a known rate from the time it is flaked until the present day. The amount of water in obsidian tools can be measured.

Tree Rings

Finally, for dating wood there is a method known as *dendrochronology*. All trees form growth rings each year, which can be seen when a tree trunk is sawn across. These rings vary in thickness according to the weather conditions and their whereabouts when they were formed. A continuous sequence of rings can be built up by starting with living trees and then working backwards through older and older pieces of timber with tree ring patterns which partly overlap with the one before. Any piece of wood from an archaeological site in a particular area with a pattern of rings which fits into this sequence can then be dated fairly exactly.

Above: Different kinds of tree pollen as seen under a microscope. The trees are labelled with their Latin names. From top to bottom they are alder, birch, hazel, horn-beam, oak and elm. Pollen grains often survive very well underground. By taking soil samples from different levels within a site and identifying the types of pollen in them, it is possible to find out what sort of vegetation covered the region around the site at various periods in the past.

Below: Restoring bronze horses at Kweilin, near Canton, China. After excavation, most bronze objects need some kind of laboratory treatment. Sometimes, as here, they just need cleaning to remove incrustations of mud or minerals which have covered the surface. In other cases part of the surface of the metal may have corroded and turned to powder. Special chemical treatment must then be used to prevent further decay.

Origins of Man

Compared with the history of the earth, the history of humans is very short. If the history of the earth filled a book with 1000 pages, the whole of our history would be on the last page. Humans belong to the group of animals called *primates*. These include apes and monkeys. Humans, however, are different from apes in three main ways: they have a bigger brain, walk upright and have greater dexterity with their hands. The separation of humans from the apes occured between 15 and 35 million years ago.

Australopithecus

The oldest known ancestors of modern human beings are called *australopithecines*. Fossil remains of these creatures have been found in many parts of Africa. The earliest remains come from the site of Lothagam in East Africa and are about 5½ million years old. The australopithecines were only about 1·2 metres (4 feet) tall and had small brains, but they walked upright. By about 2 million years ago there were at least three different types, or *species*, of australopithecines living in East Africa. One of these, called *Homo habilis*, 'handy man', probably made the first stone tools. These types of tool are called *Olduwan*, because they were first found at Olduvai Gorge, an important site in Tanzania, East Africa.

The tools were very simple, and were generally made by chipping flakes from pebbles found in stream beds. Tool-making marks an important point in human evolution. We know that *Homo habilis* could plan what he wanted to do because he made special tools to perform specific tasks, in advance. No animal except *Homo* is capable of planning his actions beforehand in this way.

By 1½ million years ago *Homo erectus*, 'upright man', had appeared. Fossil remains of *Homo erectus* have come from various parts of the world, including Africa, Java and China. Excavations at Choukoutien, near Peking in China have produced evidence which shows that *Homo erectus* used fire, hunted large animals and made more complicated stone tools. Possible remains of *Homo erectus* have also been found in Europe, at Heidelberg in Germany, and Vértesszölös in Hungary. These *Homo erectus* fossils date from between 300,000 and 400,000 years ago.

By 250,000 years ago the first early modern men and women were probably living in Europe. Like us, they belonged to the species called *Homo sapiens*, 'wise man'. An important site where early *Homo sapiens* has been found is Swanscombe, in Britain. Among the tools discovered with the human fossils there, were flint hand axes. Flint is a hard stone which is very good for making flaked stone tools. Hand axes are usually oval or pear-shaped and have an average length of 15 centimetres (6 inches).

The Stone Age

All these early stages of human development belong to the part of the Old Stone Age called the *Lower Palaeolithic* period. During this period there were many climatic changes. About one million years ago the first of

Above: Painting of a bison from the cave of Altamira in North Spain. The Altamira paintings were first discovered in 1879. The artists mainly painted large animals which they hunted for food. Possibly they thought that by painting the animals they held some sort of magical power over them, and would have greater success in hunting. Well over a hundred decorated caves have so far been discovered in France and Spain.

Below: Archaeological sites in Africa and Eurasia where remains of the Palaeolithic period have been found. Some of the finest and best explored sites are in France and Spain.

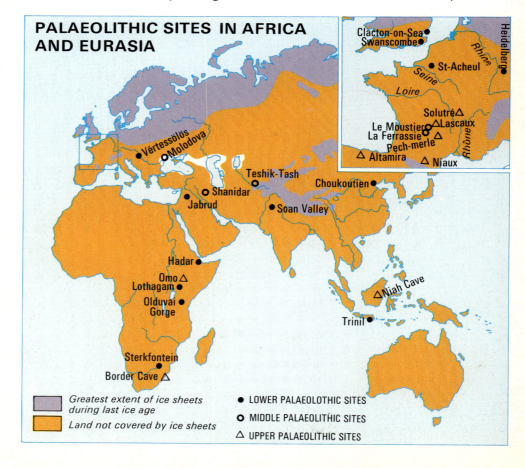

PALAEOLITHIC SITES IN AFRICA AND EURASIA

14

four great Ice Ages began. During the Ice Ages thick sheets of ice spread from the Arctic and high mountains like the Alps and covered much of North America and northern Europe. The early men from Swanscombe lived between the second and third Ice Ages.

The last Ice Age began about 70,000 years ago. During its early stages Europe and other parts of the world were inhabited by groups of humans called *Neanderthals*. Neanderthals looked rather different from us today. They had large eyebrow ridges which protruded over their eyes and receding chins and foreheads. However their brains were the same size as ours. They lived in caves and rock shelters and buried their dead, often in the floors of their homes and their stone tools were more advanced. The period of Neanderthal man is called the *Middle Palaeolithic* period. The Neanderthals disappeared about 40,000 years ago. They were replaced by a population indistinguishable from ourselves.

Cave Dwellers

The next 30,000 years is called the *Upper Palaeolithic* period. Much is known about this period, especially in Europe. Where possible, people regularly lived in rock shelters or cave entrances, as in South-west France and North Spain. In areas where there were no caves, they built large huts or tents in the open air. Excavations of these open air sites have revealed remains of ancient fireplaces which must have been used to heat the huts. They were probably also used for cooking. For food, people gathered various plants and hunted the large animals which roamed around the great grasslands of Europe and Asia, South of the ice sheets. These animals included woolly mammoths, reindeer, bison and horses.

Early Painters

Upper Palaeolithic men and women made many different tools from stone, bone, antler and ivory, and invented the bow and arrow. Most of the tools were probably used in hunting and gathering and for processing meat, skins, plants and so on. The earliest known art dates from this period. People made engravings and carvings, mostly of animals, in bone antler, ivory and stone. They also painted life-like scenes of animals on cave walls. These beautiful paintings are the most spectacular and attractive remains of early *Homo sapiens*.

Horse hunting at the site of Solutré in France during the Upper Palaeolithic period. Archaeologists discovered over 10,000 horse carcasses at the foot of the cliff. Because of this it has been suggested that the Upper Palaeolithic hunters surrounded the herds of horses on the plateau above, causing them to stampede and throw themselves over the edge of the cliff. Men waiting at the bottom probably then stripped the flesh from the animals, using flint tools, before eating it.

First Farmers

One of the most important developments in human history first took place in the Near East, in the mountainous areas and grasslands of Iran, Iraq, Turkey and the Levant. The Levant is the geographical name used to describe Palestine, Lebanon and northwest Syria. Some time after the last Ice Age, groups of people in these regions began deliberately to cultivate certain plants instead of gathering them in the wild, and to breed certain animals in captivity instead of hunting them. This marks the beginning of the *Neolithic Period*. When plants and animals are domesticated, certain changes take place in the structure of their cells. These can be recognized by specialists who study the seeds and bones from archaeological sites. These changes, however, take a long time, so we cannot be sure exactly when agriculture and animal breeding first began.

The scientific evidence shows that by around 7000 BC certain animals and plants had definitely been domesticated. People in some areas must have started to cultivate plants and breed animals long before this, for example, at Jericho, in the Jordan valley, which in about 8000 BC suddenly developed into a town covering 3–4 hectares (10 acres). The people built a massive stone wall enclosing the whole town. To do this must have required good planning, a large force of workmen and enough extra wealth to pay them. Some of this wealth probably came from trade.

Between 7000 BC and 6000 BC early farming villages grew up in many parts of the Near East. From Cayönü in South-east Turkey comes the earliest evidence for the use of copper. The people made small tools and ornaments by simply hammering out the copper. Copper was easy to get because the site is only 20 kilometres (13 miles) from a copper mine.

Jericho

The town of Jericho had grown larger by this time. New people had come to the site. They built rectangular houses with plastered floors, often painted red. In the early 1950s, Dame Kathleen Kenyon attempted to solve the problems of excavating such a vast site. She employed the local poor – the rates of pay started at two shillings a day and soared to the princely sum of five shillings a day for

Circular stone tower built against the inside of the town wall at Jericho some time after 8000 BC. The tower still stands 10 metres (30 feet) high and is about 10 metres wide at the top. There was a stairway inside it which was entered from the town. Presumably the tower and walls of Jericho were built for defence, although the identity of Jericho's enemies remains a mystery.

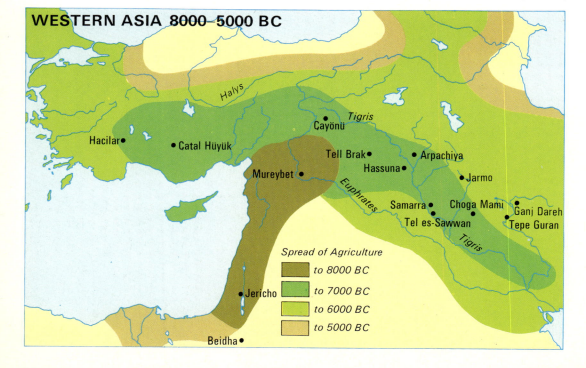

WESTERN ASIA 8000–5000 BC

Halys
Çayönü
Tigris
Hacilar
Çatal Hüyük
Tell Brak
Arpachiya
Hassuna
Mureybet
Euphrates
Jarmo
Samarra
Choga Mami
Ganj Dareh
Tel es-Sawwan
Tepe Guran
Tigris

Spread of Agriculture

- to 8000 BC
- to 7000 BC
- to 6000 BC
- to 5000 BC

Jericho

Beidha

The spread of agriculture in the Near East during the Neolithic period, from its early beginnings in the Levant and Northern Syria down to about 5000 BC when farming settlements are found throughout most of the region. Some of the important Neolithic sites which have been excavated by archaeologists are marked.

a skilled man. With her team, which included 54 field supervisors, 3 photographers, 4 technical assistants, 3 draughtsmen, a Registrar and her 6 assistants, 4 anthropologists, 4 camp supervisors, a journalist and visiting experts – she was gradually able to piece together the history of Jericho.

One of her most interesting discoveries was a group of ten human skulls on which the faces had been modelled in clay and the eyes inset with cowrie shells. Perhaps these skulls were used in ancestor worship. Other finds from Jericho included obsidian and greenstones from Turkey, turquoise from Sinai and cowrie shells from the Red Sea, showing that trade took place with these people.

At the site of Beidha, south of Jericho, many workshops were found, showing that some people specialized in different trades and crafts. One room was a butcher's shop, another was used by a maker of stone tools, another by a bead-maker and so on. Tools, raw materials and half-finished products were found in all these workshops.

An important site in the foothills of the Zagros mountains is Jarmo, where large quantities of pottery appear for the first time. Pottery is very useful for archaeologists. When the same type of pottery is found on different sites, for example, this shows that the sites are of approximately the

same date and that they were in some sort of direct or indirect contact with each other.

Between 6000 BC and 5000 BC a village, Catal Hüyük, established itself on the Konya plain in Turkey. This village became the largest known Neolithic site in the Near East. It covered over 12 hectares (32 acres) and probably had a population of 5000–6000. The houses were made of timber and mud brick and were built against one another. There were no streets, so people walked along the flat roofs, which had openings in them to enter the houses. The skeletons of the dead were wrapped in cloth and buried in the houses, under platforms which were used for sleeping on! Many buildings at Çatal Hüyük were probably holy places used for worshipping the gods. They were decorated with wall paintings or figures modelled in plaster.

At sites such as Tell es-Sawwan and Choga Mami in Iraq, early *irrigation* agriculture was probably practised. This means that water was brought to the fields along artificial channels. The development of irrigation marks another very important step in human history, because with irrigation it was possible to cultivate the fertile plains of southern Iraq. This provided the conditions which led to the growth of one of the world's earliest civilizations, ancient Sumer.

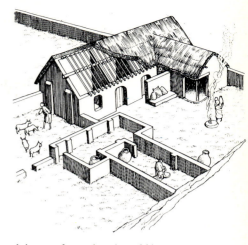

A house from the site of Hassuna in northern Iraq, around 5000 BC. Hassuna was a small farming village, probably like those which dot the plain of northern Iraq today. The houses were built of packed mud and had several rooms opening on to a courtyard in which were ovens, grain bins and so on.

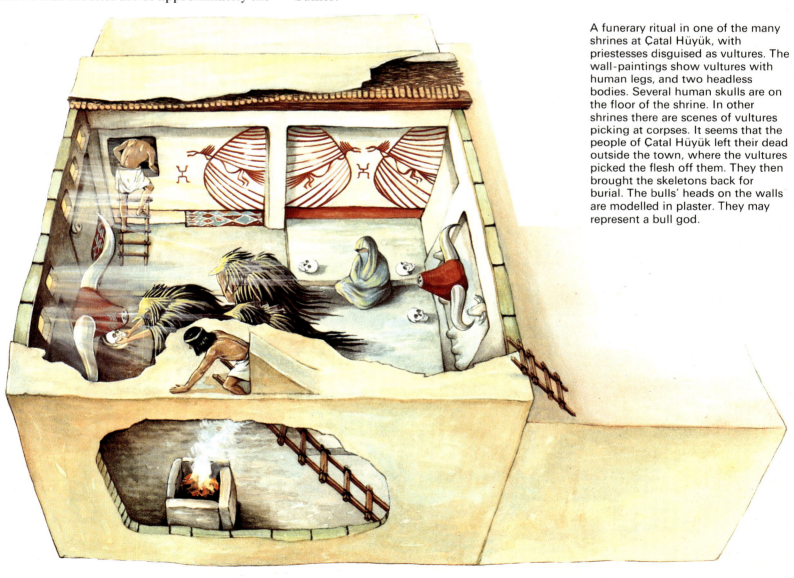

A funerary ritual in one of the many shrines at Çatal Hüyük, with priestesses disguised as vultures. The wall-paintings show vultures with human legs, and two headless bodies. Several human skulls are on the floor of the shrine. In other shrines there are scenes of vultures picking at corpses. It seems that the people of Çatal Hüyük left their dead outside the town, where the vultures picked the flesh off them. They then brought the skeletons back for burial. The bulls' heads on the walls are modelled in plaster. They may represent a bull god.

Early Western Asia

By 3000 BC the civilization of ancient Sumer was flourishing in Southern Iraq. The region was divided up into many small states, each controlled by a particular city. The temple, the home of the city god, was a central feature of every Sumerian city. Originally these *city states* were perhaps governed by the temple authorities, but soon control passed to secular rulers. Early palaces, where these rulers lived, have been excavated at sites such as Eridu and Kish.

One of the greatest Sumerian achievements was the invention of a writing system. Writing was invented as a method of bookkeeping, and the earliest texts are lists of animals and farm equipment. The writing was pressed into clay tablets with a *stylus* or pen, made of wood or reed. Because the end of the stylus was cut in the shape of a thin wedge, it made a series of wedge-shaped marks in the clay. From early picture shapes a series of signs developed which were used to write the syllables of words. This wedge-shaped writing is called *cuneiform*, because

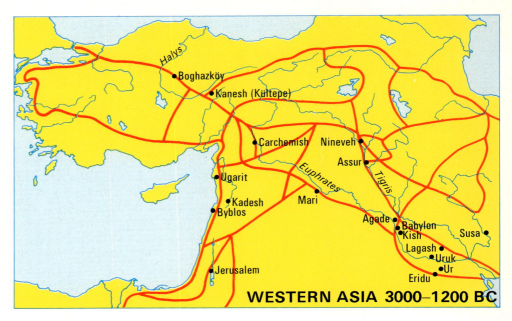

WESTERN ASIA 3000–1200 BC

Above: The Near East during the Bronze Age, showing the important Sumerian, Babylonian, Assyrian and Hittite sites and trade routes.

Below: Rock carving from Yazilikaya, an open air rock sanctuary near the Hittite capital of Boghazköy. It shows the Hittite king Tudhaliya IV dressed in a mantle and shawl and carrying a long crook. The name Tudhaliya is carved beside the figure in Hittite hieroglyphs. At Yazilikaya two great processions of 70 gods and goddeses are carved into the rock.

the Latin word for wedge is *cuneus*. The cuneiform script was later used by other peoples in the Near East for writing their own languages. In the same way our own script is used for writing many European languages other than English, such as, for example, French, German and Italian.

Tablets with cuneiform writing were extremely common, but nobody could read them. Sir Henry Rawlinson (1810–95), an officer in the East India Company's Army, was sent to reorganize the Persian Army. While there he became interested in cuneiform inscriptions. One day he was at Behistun, visiting the tombs of the early kings of Persia, when high up on a cliff, he spotted an immense inscription. At considerable risk he climbed the cliff and copied it. On his return he found that it was written in three different languages – Old Persian, Elamite and Akkadian. Rawlinson managed to decipher the Old Persian first. This was the key to the other two languages.

We can learn many different things about the Sumerians from the cuneiform texts. We know, for example, that they travelled far and wide in search of metals, woods, stones and other rare materials.

The first great age of Sumer came to an end in 2340 BC with the rise of King Sargon, who established his capital city at Agade, in the north of Sumer. Sargon was not Sumerian. He spoke Akkadian, which is a *Semitic* language, like modern Arabic and Hebrew. After the fall of Sargon's dynasty there was a short revival of Sumerian civilization, under kings who ruled from the city of Ur. They carried out great building programmes, and archaeologists have uncovered the remains of many palaces and temples of this period. In some of the temple precincts were monuments known as *ziggurats*, stepped towers which probably had a small shrine at the top.

Babylonians

Semitic-speaking invaders from the west played a part in putting an end to this last

Above: Clay tablet with cuneiform writing. There are many different kinds of cuneiform documents, including letters, legal and administrative documents, religious texts and historical records. The tablets vary in size and shape, but the most common form was rectangular and of a size easy to hold in the hand.

Below: A classroom at Mari, based on the excavations, with rows of clay benches for the students, in the royal palace. Tablets were made from wet clay in the round containers. The teacher then wrote on part of the tablet, and the student tried to copy the example. Many of these school tablets have been found on sites throughout Mesopotamia.

Sumerian dynasty around 2000 BC. In several cities new dynasties were founded, the most famous of which was that of Babylon, near modern Baghdad, founded in 1894 BC.

One of the kings of this dynasty was Hammurabi. He is famous as the author of one of the earliest known law codes, which was inscribed on a black stone *stele* – a type of pillar. At the top is a carving of Hammurabi himself, standing before the sun god Shamash, who was the god of justice. The laws cover many things, including agricultural disputes, family law and penalties for crimes such as murder.

Babylon was just one of many kingdoms at this time. Their rulers lived in luxury in enormous palaces. For example, the one excavated at Mari, on the River Euphrates, had more than 260 rooms and courts, many with colourful wall paintings. More than 13,000 cuneiform tablets were found at Mari, giving a day-to-day view of events of the time unequalled in the ancient world.

In the north of Iraq was the land of Assyria, with its capital at Assur on the River Tigris. Merchants from Assur traded extensively with Anatolia (modern Turkey) at this period. They sent tin and textiles by donkey caravan across the mountains to Assyrian agents livng in the Anatolian towns. These agents sold the goods at a good profit to the local people.

Hittites

Soon afterwards a new power arose in Anatolia. This was the Hittite Kingdom, with its capital at Boghazköy. Boghazköy was a huge city, surrounded by a massive defensive wall of stone and mud brick. Many cuneiform tablets have been found there written mostly in Hittite. Hittite belongs to the group of languages known as *Indo-European*. Most modern European languages, including English, are Indo-European, and are related to Hittite. Some words have hardly changed. The Hittite word for water, for example, was *watar*. The Hittites became a great military power, and by 1300 BC had a large empire which covered much of Turkey and northern Syria. This was an age of powerful states and international politics in the Near East. But in about 1200 BC the Hittite empire collapsed and the other great powers, especially Egypt, had severe problems partly caused by a sudden and great movement of peoples.

The Nile Valley

Above: The development of pyramid building. 1. At first, kings and nobles were buried in a *mastaba*, a pit in the sand above which was built a mud brick structure shaped like a bench. 2. The first step pyramid was at Saqqara. It was changed several times during construction. A small step pyramid was built over the original mastaba. This was then extended and the whole encased in limestone. 3. This pyramid at Meydum started as a step pyramid but finally the steps were filled in with local stone and faced with limestone to make a smooth surface. 4. True pyramid of King Khufu (Kheops) at Giza, the largest pyramid in Egypt.

In the late prehistoric period Egypt was divided into two kingdoms. In the North was the kingdom of *Lower Egypt*, which included the delta of the River Nile, a fertile plain formed of river mud. In the South was the kingdom of *Upper Egypt*, which stretched along the Nile valley. These two kingdoms were eventually united in 3200 BC, under the first *Pharaoh*, Menes. From this time onwards, a unified kingdom was the ideal of most Egyptians. Nevertheless there were changes in the course of Egyptian history, and long periods of stable rule by the central government were interrupted by periods of disorder.

The Egyptian pharaoh was a god-king. During his lifetime he was thought to be the great sun god, Horus, on earth. When he died he became Osiris, the god of the dead, and his son took his place as the new Horus. The pharaohs made elaborate preparations for their death. They wished to be buried in tombs that would last for ever. Construction of these tombs usually began at the begin-

ning of each new reign.

During the *Old Kingdom* (c.2660–2180 BC) great *pyramids* were built to house the bodies of the pharaohs. Many of these pyramids can still be seen in Egypt, and they have been carefully investigated by archaeologists. The largest is the pyramid of Kheops at Giza, near Cairo, a spectacular piece of engineering even by today's standards. It was over 146 metres (480 feet) high and more than 2 million huge limestone blocks were used in its construction. Near the pyramids were the tombs of other members of the royal family and various officials and courtiers. The main capital of the Old Kingdom was Memphis, the walls of which were said to have been built by Menes.

The pharaohs of the *Middle Kingdom* (c.2080–1640 BC) originated from Thebes in Upper Egypt which thus became an important political centre, but they also built a new capital, at Itj-Towy, near ancient Memphis. They extended the frontiers of Egypt as far south as the second Nile cataract, and built large fortresses along the river to protect the trading ships which brought gold and luxury products to Egypt from Nubia and the Sudan.

The Glint of Gold

The pharaohs of the *New Kingdom* (c. 1570–1075 BC) also ruled from Thebes. They were buried in splendid rock-cut tombs in a desert valley on the west bank of the Nile,

The mortuary temple of Sahure, one of the Old Kingdom pharaohs, at Abusir. When a pharaoh died, his coffin was brought along the river to his mortuary temple. The coffin was dragged up the causeway from the temple to the pyramid where the pharaoh was laid to rest in the burial chamber surrounded by his splendid possessions. After this, daily rituals were performed in the mortuary temple, which was dedicated to a particular god.

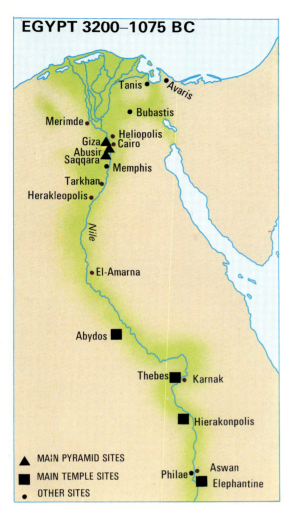

EGYPT 3200–1075 BC

- Tanis
- Avaris
- Merimde
- Bubastis
- Heliopolis
- Giza
- Cairo
- Abusir
- Saqqara
- Memphis
- Tarkhan
- Herakleopolis
- Nile
- El-Amarna
- Abydos
- Thebes
- Karnak
- Hierakonpolis
- Philae
- Aswan
- Elephantine

▲ MAIN PYRAMID SITES
■ MAIN TEMPLE SITES
• OTHER SITES

Left: The Nile Valley with important ancient Egyptian sites. The area shaded green is the fertile agricultural land along the river. Once every year, in late summer, the Nile flooded laying down rich black mud on the land. Because of the colour of this mud the ancient Egyptians called their country *Kmt* – 'the Black Land'. On either side of the narrow fertile strip is the desert, which they called *Dšrt* – 'the Red Land'.

Below: Restoration work at the temple of Queen Hatshepsut, Deir el-Bahri, part of ancient Thebes. Queen Hatshepsut was a remarkable woman. She was the daughter of the pharaoh Tuthmosis I and wife of Tuthmosis II. When her husband died, she seized the throne for herself and ruled Egypt as pharaoh. In the scenes in her beautiful temple at Deir el-Bahri, which was designed by the royal architect and favourite Senenmut, Hatshepsut tries to justify her actions. She is shown being crowned as rightful ruler of Egypt by her royal father. She is also described as 'son' of god, and various paintings show her divine birth.

part of ancient Thebes. One pharaoh, Akhenaten, tried to introduce the worship of a single god, Aten, into Egypt. Aten was represented as the sun, with its rays ending in tiny hands. Akhenaten moved his capital to a new site at Tell el-Amarna, where he built temples to Aten which were open to the sky. After Akhenaten's death, however, his successors returned to the old religion.

One of the most important Egyptian professions was that of the *scribe*. Scribes were educated in schools attached to palaces or temples where they learned to write the Egyptian *hieroglyphic* script. Scribal training was necessary for important posts in administration and the army and for careers in such professions as the priesthood, medicine and art and architecture.

Most Egyptians were uneducated peasants who worked in the fields alongside the River Nile. Agricultural scenes painted on tomb walls show the everyday life of the Egyptian farmers. Other paintings depict the activities of craftsmen and labourers who lived in the towns. A whole community of such workers lived for nearly four centuries at Deir el-Medina near the Valley of the Kings, employed mostly on the construction and decoration of the tombs of the pharaohs. The lowest social class, however, were the slaves. Many slaves were captives taken in war, and they worked in the temples and palaces and on private estates.

opposite the city. Today this is called the *Valley of the Kings*. Archaeologists have investigated all these tombs. The walls are beautifully decorated with paintings which show many different aspects of ancient Egyptian life and religion. Unfortunately robbers stole most of the contents of the ancient tombs long before the days of modern archaeology. However, in 1922, the English archaeologist, Howard Carter, working for Lord Carnarvon, discovered one tomb which had not been robbed. This was the tomb of Tutankhamun, a fairly unimportant pharaoh who only reigned for nine years. Tutankhamun's remarkable burial equipment can only make us wonder at what the tombs of greater pharaohs, which were much larger and more elaborately decorated, must once have contained. So much splendid treasure was buried with Tutankhamun that it took three years for the archaeologists to clear and preserve the contents of the tomb. The New Kingdom was a golden age in Egyptian history and many new temples were built. The country was stable and wealthy, and the pharaohs controlled an empire stretching from the Sudan in the south to Syria in the north.

Archaeologists have excavated the remains of many of these temples. They were impressive buildings with forecourts, columned halls, sanctuaries and monumental gateways decorated with scenes and texts. One of the largest and most famous is the great temple of the god Amun at Karnak,

The Great Granary on the citadel at Mohenjo-daro, made of timber and mud brick. The open passages left in the brickwork below the grain storage area allowed the air to circulate freely. Grain was probably brought into Mohenjo-daro from the countryside as some kind of state tax. It was then stored in the granary and probably distributed as wages to government workers.

Indus Valley

The first civilization of ancient India, with its main settlements in the valleys of the River Indus and its tributaries, is called the *Indus civilization*. Sometimes it is called the *Harappan civilization*, after one of the most important sites, Harappa. It developed out of the earlier Neolithic cultures in the hills and valleys of Afghanistan and Baluchistan to the West. By 2300 BC some farming communities were living in the alluvial plain of the Indus, at sites such as Amri and Kot Diji. This early settlement in the Indus valley is called *pre-Harappan*. The remains of the Indus culture have been excavated from on top of the pre-Harappan levels at these sites, and new settlements appear throughout the region.

Over 150 sites are known in an area of almost 1·3 million square kilometres ($\frac{1}{2}$ million square miles). This makes the Indus civilization the largest known Bronze Age civilization in the world. Two sites, Harappa and Mohenjo-daro, are much larger than the others. They were probably the main administrative centres. 30,000–40,000 people lived in each city. Smaller towns, like Kalibangan, Chanhu-daro and Lothal were perhaps local centres of government. Most Indus sites, however, were villages.

A hieroglyphic writing system was used by the Indus people, but unfortunately no one, so far, has been able to decipher it. All the inscriptions are on seals and are very short. Presumably they wrote mostly on some perishable material, perhaps wood, which has long since decayed. Therefore all our information about the Indus civilization comes from archaeology.

The Archaeologists
Many Indus sites have been excavated. The British archaeologists Sir John Marshall and E. Mackay employed hundreds of workmen to dig the huge mound of Mohenjo-daro between 1922 and 1931. After the war further work was done there by Sir Mortimer Wheeler, who also excavated Harappa. At both sites a high mound or citadel on the West looked over the lower town, where a network of streets intersected the blocks of houses. On or near the mounds were important buildings. The Great Bath at Mohenjo-daro was perhaps used for ritual bathing – in many Indian temples today there are large tanks of holy water where people bathe to purify themselves. Next to the Great Bath was a huge granary for storing corn. The

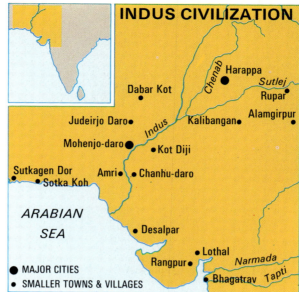

INDUS CIVILIZATION

● MAJOR CITIES
● SMALLER TOWNS & VILLAGES

This map shows the major archaeological sites of the Indus civilization, most of which are in present day Pakistan. The Indus civilization covered an area greater than any other known Bronze Age civilization. The same kinds of pottery and other objects, the same type of architecture and town planning and the same sized bricks are found throughout the whole area. This suggests very efficient organization, perhaps from a central government.

remains of granaries were also found near the mound at Harappa, together with rows of circular brick platforms for threshing grain. The smaller towns also had citadels. One of the buildings on the citadel at Kalibangan may have been a temple. In one room, there were structures which archaeologists think may have been fire altars. Even the villages had a small citadel. We do not know what was built on them because no villages have been excavated.

The houses of the general population were in the lower town. These varied in size from one-roomed dwellings for the poor to great houses with many rooms and courtyards for the rich. Most large houses had a private well, hearths to heat the rooms and a bathroom with a drainage channel leading to the main street drain. All towns had a very efficient drainage system. There were many workshops in the lower towns, including metal workers', shell-ornament makers' and bead makers' shops, dyers' vats and potters' kilns. The products from these centres were traded throughout the Indus area. For trading a standard system of weights and measures was used. Many stone weights have been found at Mohenjo-daro and other sites. The lovely Indus seals, which depict real and imaginary animals, were also used in trading. They were pressed into the clay which was used to seal bales of merchandise

and then removed, leaving an impression in the clay. A few of these seals have been found as far away as southern Iraq. The Indus people traded with ancient Sumer through the trading centre of Dilmun, the modern island of Bahrain in the Arabian Gulf. It is often mentioned in Sumerian cuneiform texts.

An Enigma

Some time around 1700 BC the towns and cities of the Indus civilization were suddenly abandoned. We do not know why this happened. Archaeologists have found no real evidence for destruction by invaders. Several skeletons found in the streets at Mohenjo-daro were once thought to be evidence for a great massacre. But we now know that they date from a time after the city had been abandoned, and was probably only occupied by some groups of 'squatters'. Many suggestions have been made to explain the decline of the Indus culture, but none of these have been generally accepted. For the moment the reasons for the end of this great civilization remain a mystery.

Two seals from Mohenjo-daro, showing an Indian rhinoceros (left) and an Indian humped bull (right). They are carved out of steatite, a hard stone which was baked to harden and glaze the surface. Above the animals are short inscriptions in the Indus script, which has not yet been deciphered. Most of the seals come from the larger Indus sites, where they were probably used in trade and administration. They mainly depict animals, but a few are carved with mythological or religious scenes.

Aegean World

'Out in the dark blue sea there lies a land called Crete, a rich and lovely land, washed by waves on every side, densely peopled and boasting 90 cities . . . One of the 90 towns is a great city called Knossos and there, for nine years, King Minos ruled.' This is how Odysseus the hero described the largest of the Greek islands to his wife in Homer's 'Odyssey'. There were many ancient legends about King Minos and Crete. The legend of Theseus and the Minotaur tells that under the palace of Knossos there was a labyrinth where lived a dreadful monster, the Minotaur, half-man and half-bull. No one who entered the labyrinth could find the way out again. Every year King Minos demanded from Athens seven youths and seven maidens to be sacrificed to the Minotaur. One year the hero Theseus, the prince of Athens, went with the other young Athenians. When he arrived in Crete, Minos' daughter, Ariadne, fell in love with him. She gave him a ball of thread which he fastened to the door of the labyrinth and unravelled as he went in search of the Minotaur, which he killed after a fierce battle. He found his way out of the maze by following the thread, and escaped from Crete with Ariadne.

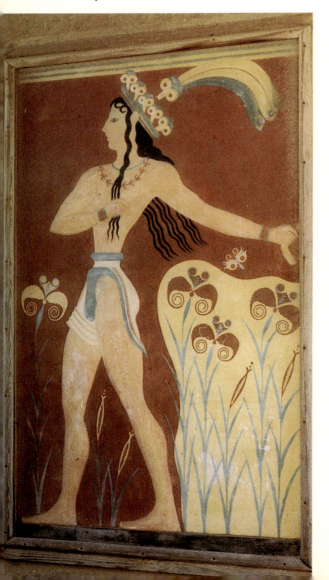

One hundred years ago no one believed there was any truth in these legends. The ancient civilization of Crete had been totally forgotten. Then, one day a young English archaeologist, Arthur Evans, found some little carved stones in an Athenian antique shop on which was some tiny indecipherable writing such as he had seen before at his museum in Oxford. He asked where the stones had been found. 'On the island of Crete', came the reply. Today, thanks to Sir Arthur Evans, we know that some 4000 or 5000 years ago there were great palaces and cities on Crete, which was the centre of the earliest known European civilization, called *Minoan* after King Minos.

The Bull God

Archaeologists have discovered four royal palaces at Knossos, Phaestos, Mallia and Zakro. They had several storeys, with large rooms, grouped round a central court and were used both for administration and for religious ceremonies. Cretan artists were very highly skilled. They made some of the most beautiful jewellery in the ancient world, and the palace walls were decorated with colourful paintings showing palace life, religion, sport and country scenery. From such finds we know for example that the Minoans worshipped a mother goddess and a young god, and sacrificed bulls to them. There were bull-leaping ceremonies in the central courts of the palaces. Young men and women would grasp the horns of a charging bull and somersault over its back.

Like other great civilizations of the time the Minoans had a writing system. Early hieroglyphs developed into a script which we call *Linear A*. It was used between 1900 BC and 1450 BC. The script, however, has yet to be deciphered. The Minoans traded with the Hittites, Syria and Egypt. We know this because a few Egyptian and Near Eastern documents refer to it and also Minoan pottery has been found on some archaeological sites in these areas. The Minoans had settlements on the Greek islands of Thera and Kythera. Archaeologists have discovered several large mansions on Thera decorated with colourful frescoes and full of household objects, such as pots beautifully decorated with motifs such as flying swallows and playing dolphins.

The Myceneans

In 1450 BC all the palaces and settlements on Crete were destroyed by a series of natural catastrophes and abandoned. Only Knossos was reoccupied, for about 50 years, but by foreigners, not native Cretans. These were *Myceneans*, from the Greek mainland, a people who had been under the influence of Crete for some time. The greatest days of Mycenean civilization came after the fall of Crete. Warrior rulers lived in palaces like those which have been excavated at Mycenae, Pylos, Thebes and Tiryns. They

Above: The Palace of Nestor at Pylos. The palace was built in c.1300 BC and completely destroyed by a great fire about 100 years later. The throne room, at the back of the palace, had a central hearth surrounded by four columns, which supported a balcony. The walls were decorated with colourful paintings, and the floor was also covered with coloured designs.

Left: Fresco from the Minoan palace at Knossos. It shows a young prince wearing a feathered crown walking in a flower garden. The fresco has been much restored, but the crown, the body and much of the left leg are original.

Below: Dome-shaped or beehive tomb at Mycenae, known as the Treasury of Atreus c.1300 BC. We do not know who was buried there because the contents had been robbed long before it was investigated by modern archaeologists.

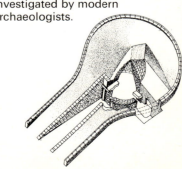

were buried in beehive-shaped stone tombs, like the Treasury of Atreus at Mycenae, together with their weapons. The Mycenaeans spoke an early dialect of Greek which they wrote on tablets in a script known as *Linear B*.

The names and deeds of many Mycenean warrior heroes have been preserved for us in the two great poems of Homer, the 'Iliad' and the 'Odyssey'. The 'Iliad' describes how Agamemnon of Mycenae and other rulers such as Menelaus of Sparta, Odysseus of Ithaca and Nestor of Pylos organized a great expedition against the city of Troy to rescue Helen, the beautiful wife of Menelaus. She had been captured by the Trojans. The *Trojan War* raged for many years. In the end the city was captured by a cunning trick. The Greeks built a huge wooden horse inside which they hid a number of their warriors. Persuaded that the horse would bring them luck, the Trojans dragged it one night into their city. The warriors came out of the horse, and opened the gates to their fellow Greeks outside. They set fire to Troy destroying the whole town.

It is impossible to know how much in these stories is fact and how much is legend. But, as a young boy, Heinrich Schliemann (1822–90), son of a poor German pastor, had read Homer's account of the attack on the walls of Troy. He thought to himself: 'If these walls existed, they must still be there. One day I shall dig them up'. By the age of 46 in 1868, through buying and selling indigo in Russia, Schliemann had amassed a huge fortune. He then set out to look for Troy. The rest is history. We now know that it was a flourishing city in Mycenean times, surrounded by massive defensive walls. But inexplicably the civilization collapsed. The ancient writers believed it was because of too much warfare between rival states. It was followed by a Dark Age in Greece, which lasted until about 800 BC.

Below: Map showing important Minoan and Mycenean sites and the extent of Mycenean civilization.

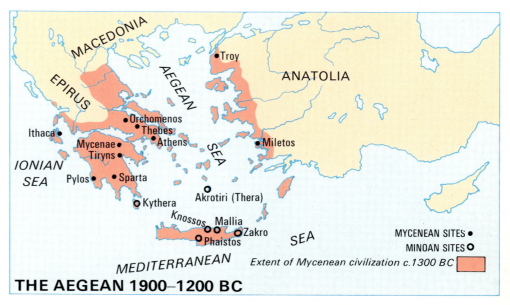

THE AEGEAN 1900–1200 BC

MYCENEAN SITES ●
MINOAN SITES ○

Extent of Mycenean civilization c.1300 BC ▮

Late Western Asia

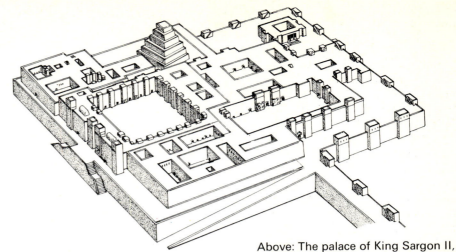

Some time after the troubles and unrest in the Near East at the end of the Bronze Age, Assyria returned as a strong and powerful nation. From about 900 BC onwards a series of Assyrian kings gradually extended their territory by military conquest. By 650 BC they controlled a huge empire which included the whole of Mesopotamia, Western Iran, the Levant, Southern Turkey and Egypt.

One of the first kings, Assur-naṣir-apli II, moved his capital from Assur to the site of Kalhu (modern Nimrud). There he built a splendid palace, overlooking the River Tigris. We know from inscriptions that when the palace was completed, he gave a huge banquet at which there were nearly 70,000 guests who were given food and drink for 10 days. The menu included 14,000 sheep and 10,000 skins of wine. Temples, fortification walls and smaller palaces for high officials and royal relatives were also built at Kalhu by Assur-naṣir-apli and later Assyrian kings.

At the height of Assyrian power, King Sargon II decided to build himself a new capital, called 'Fort Sargon' (modern Khorsabad). Many deported prisoners of war were used for this great building project. But after Sargon's death his son, Sennacherib, decided to rule from the ancient city of Nineveh, which remained the capital until the fall of Assyria.

The courtyards and main rooms of Assyrian palaces were lined with limestone blocks carved with scenes of the king's military triumphs and the royal lion hunt. Many of the inner rooms were decorated with ritual scenes and there were huge winged bulls at the palace gates which were thought to give supernatural protection. Archaeologists have also found tribute from the lands under Assyrian control, especially bronzes and ivory carvings, in many palace rooms.

Above: The palace of King Sargon II, completed in 707 BC. Stone winged bulls and other figures guarded the three entrances to the throne room. There were three small temples attached to the palace. A small ziggurat adjoined these temples. Each stage of the ziggurat was painted a different colour.

Below: Staircase leading up to the great columned audience hall, or *adapana*, of Darius I at Persepolis. The sculptured reliefs on the stairway show the famous 'Immortals', the supreme royal guard of 10,000 foot soldiers. At the front of the staircase Median and Persian guards are shown standing below the winged disc of Ahuramazda. On either side of them are panels with a lion attacking a bull, an ancient symbol associated with royalty. A few of the many columns are now standing.

The last great Assyrian king, Assur-ban-apli, thought of himself as a great scholar, and he describes proudly how he learned to read, write and solve mathematical problems. He collected a great library of cuneiform tablets in Nineveh, which was discovered by archaeologists excavating the city. The king always consulted the gods before taking any important decision. For this there were specialists who could read the omens. Many letters from such priests also advise the king on how to prevent misfortune after unnatural happenings, such as the eclipse of the sun.

Babylonia

Less than 20 years after Assur-ban-apli's death, Babylon took Assyria's place as the greatest power in the Near East. King Nebuchadnezzar controlled an empire almost as large as that of Assyria. The Bible tells us of his capture of Jerusalem and how he carried off King Zedekiah and much of the city's population to exile in Babylon. He wanted to make Babylon the greatest city in the world and in his inscriptions he describes the building of its walls, temples and palaces. According to the Greeks, Nebuchadnezzar built one of the seven wonders of the world, the *Hanging Gardens*, for a princess from the East. But the Babylonian Empire only lasted a short time.

The last king, Nabonidus, was much more interested in religion than in administration or military affairs. For ten years, he left his son, Belshazzar, to govern Babylonia, while he lived as a hermit in an oasis in the Arabian desert. Shortly after his return, Babylonia was invaded by the Persian army under Cyrus. In 539 BC, Babylon was captured and Nabonidus was taken prisoner.

Persia

All the provinces of the Babylonian empire then submitted to Cyrus. But under Darius the Great, the empire grew to its greatest extent, stretching from Libya to Central Asia and from south-east Europe to India. Cyrus founded a new imperial capital at Pasargadae where he was buried in a large tomb. At Persepolis, to the south, Darius built a huge ceremonial centre. On a high stone terrace were many monumental buildings, decorated with relief sculptures. Among these was a large, columned audience hall where the king received envoys from the different parts of his empire. The main god of the Persians was Ahuramazda, who is shown as a figure within a winged disc. They also practised fire-worship.

The Persian kings ruled justly and they allowed the provinces to keep their own local laws, customs and traditions. Each province had a governor, or *satrap*. But in 334 BC, Alexander the Great crossed into Asia, and four years later he burned down Persepolis. The last Persian king, Artaxerxes IV, who had mustered his troops in the East, was finally defeated in 327 BC.

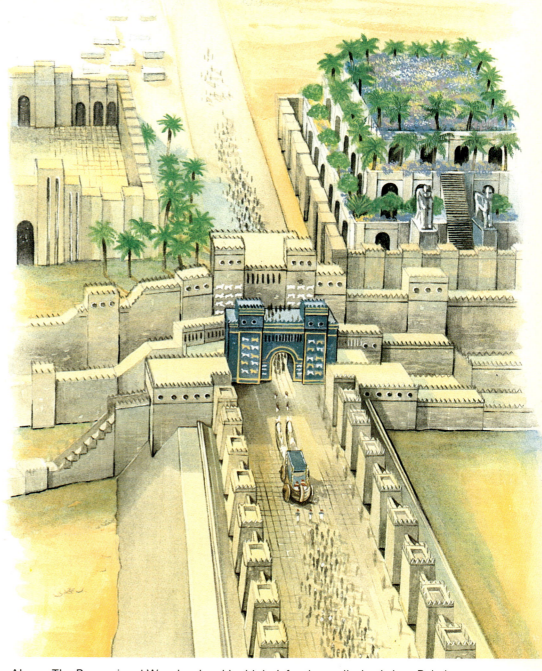

Above: The Processional Way, bordered by high defensive walls, leads into Babylon through the Ištar Gate which was ornamented with glazed brick animals and rosettes. Inside the city to the left is the temple of the mother goddess, Ninmah. To the right is part of the royal palace of Nebuchadnezzar, with the Hanging Gardens.

Below: This map of the Near East shows the maximum extent of the great empires of Assyria, Babylonia and Persia, and some of the major archaeological sites.

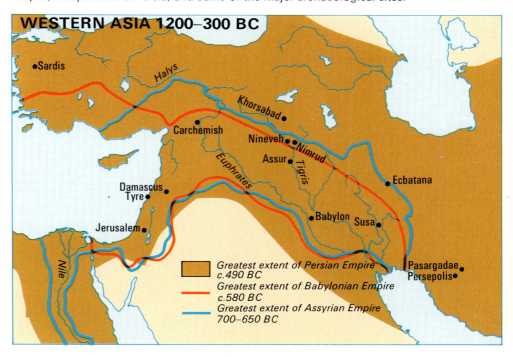

WESTERN ASIA 1200–300 BC

Greatest extent of Persian Empire c.490 BC
Greatest extent of Babylonian Empire c.580 BC
Greatest extent of Assyrian Empire 700–650 BC

Sardis · Halys · Khorsabad · Carchemish · Nineveh · Nimrud · Assur · Tigris · Euphrates · Ecbatana · Damascus · Tyre · Babylon · Susa · Jerusalem · Nile · Pasargadae · Persepolis

Classical Greece

The *Classical Age* of Greece began in about 500 BC. In the centuries before this – the *Archaic Period* – many Greeks moved away from their homeland because there was too little farmland to support the growing population. They founded new colonies throughout the North Mediterranean, from Spain in the West to the Black Sea in the East. Many of these colonies grew rich and prosperous.

Greece itself was divided into many independent *city states*, with different forms of government and different traditions. Two of the most powerful states were Athens and Sparta. Sparta was a land of severe customs, designed to produce great warriors. Any male babies who were weak and sickly were taken into the mountains and left there to die. All other boys were taken from their mothers at the age of seven and brought up together in groups. They had no extra clothes for winter and they were given only a kind of wheat porridge to eat. Young adult men continued to live together. They passed their lives in military training, hunting and supervising the serfs on their farms. They could only visit their wives in secret. Girls also had an athletic training, to make them fit to be the mothers of warriors.

By the Classical Period, Athens had a democratic form of government, with an Assembly where every Athenian citizen had the right to vote. The business for the Assembly was prepared by the *Council of Five Hundred*, made up of representatives from the various districts of the Athenian state.

The Parthenon

We know a lot about Classical Athens, both from archaeological excavations and from what the Greeks themselves wrote at the time. Many of the beautiful buildings which can be seen today on the *acropolis* date to this period. These include the *Parthenon*, which was a temple to Athena, the patron goddess of the city. All around the Parthenon was a sculptured frieze, the work of Pheidias, one of the most gifted artists of the day. Pheidias also made a gold and ivory statue of Athena, which stood inside the temple, but this has long since disappeared.

Every four years, Greeks gathered at Olympia for a week of games. During the festival, city states which were at war with each other honoured a truce. Many of the games, such as the race here, run by soldiers, or *hoplites*, in full kit, took place in the great Olympic stadium, which has been excavated by archaeologists, and can be seen today.

View of the acropolis at Athens with the Parthenon, the great temple to the goddess Athena, in the foreground. It was built between 447 and 432 BC. Many of the sculptures which once ornamented the Parthenon are now in the British Museum. At each end of the building were scenes from Athenian mythology – the birth of the goddess Athena and the dispute between Athena and the god Poseidon for the patronage of Athens. Around the sides were figures of gods and heroes.

Elgin Marbles

In 1799, Lord Elgin went to Turkey as British Ambassador. Turkey then ruled Greece. There Lord Elgin found the Parthenon half ruined. Elgin decided to rescue its marbles. The beautiful 'Elgin Marbles' were sent to Britain, where they sit, in the British Museum. Some people think they should be returned to Greece. When Elgin returned, he thought to have the sculptures retouched. He approached Canova, a great sculptor of the day. But, thankfully, he refused with the words: 'It would be sacrilege in me, or any man, to presume to touch them with a chisel'.

Below the acropolis was the *agora*, or market place. Every sort of thing could be bought in the agora, and many craftsmen had their houses there, with workshops attached. Sometimes the central area was cleared for the performance of plays. Famous teachers like Socrates spent much time in the agora discussing problems with groups of pupils.

Sparta and other states in that part of Greece, which is known as the *Peloponnese*, began to be afraid of the growth of Athenian power. A major war, called the *Peloponnesian War*, broke out in 431 BC. The Greek Historian, Thucydides, has left us a long account of this war.

Afterwards power passed to Sparta, and later to Thebes, but neither succeeded in unifying the whole of Greece. Athens was still the home of artists and great scholars, including Plato and his pupil Aristotle. Aristotle was the tutor of Alexander the Great, son of Philip of Macedonia, a kingdom in Northern Greece. It was the Macedonians, first under Philip and then under Alexander, who conquered mainland Greece, the Greek islands and then Asia and Egypt. With these conquests the Classical Age of Greece came to an end.

Above: The god Hermes holding the young god Dionysus. It was carved by the famous sculptor Praxiteles (c.340 BC). The sculpture once stood inside the temple of the goddess Hera at Olympia.

Below: This map shows some of the many archaeological sites of Classical Greece. Greece was divided up into numerous small city states at this period. Each state was named after its capital city. The smallest states were little bigger than the city itself.

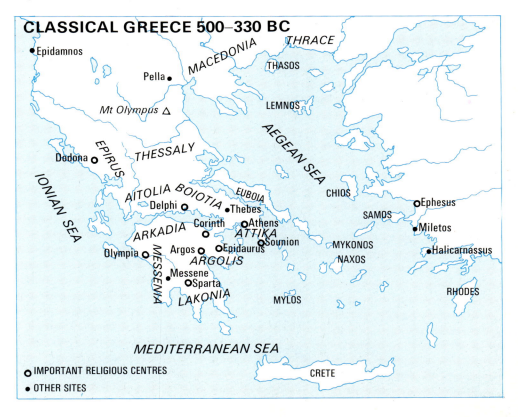

CLASSICAL GREECE 500–330 BC

o IMPORTANT RELIGIOUS CENTRES
• OTHER SITES

Prehistoric Europe

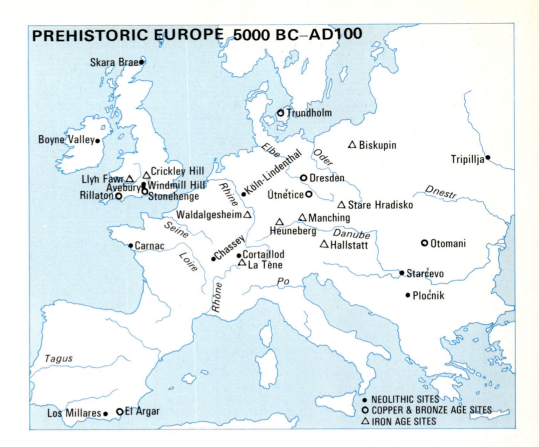

PREHISTORIC EUROPE 5000 BC–AD100

- Skara Brae
- Trundholm
- Boyne Valley
- Biskupin
- Tripillja
- Crickley Hill
- Köln-Lindenthal
- Oder
- Elbe
- Llyn Fawr
- Windmill Hill
- Dresden
- Dnestr
- Avebury
- Rillaton
- Stonehenge
- Útnetice
- Stare Hradisko
- Rhine
- Waldalgesheim
- Manching
- Seine
- Heuneberg
- Danube
- Otomani
- Carnac
- Chassey
- Cortaillod
- La Tène
- Hallstatt
- Starčevo
- Loire
- Po
- Pločnik
- Rhône
- Tagus
- Los Millares
- El Argar

● NEOLITHIC SITES
○ COPPER & BRONZE AGE SITES
△ IRON AGE SITES

During the Neolithic Period, which began in several areas of Europe some time around 5000 BC, Europe was the home of many groups of people. Almost all the information we have about these people comes from archaeology. They lived in farming settlements where they grew cereals and other crops and kept domesticated animals. In different parts of Europe people had different customs and traditions. For example, in South-east Europe they lived in one-roomed wooden houses. Further north the houses had several rooms and were arranged in circles around two larger buildings. In central Europe people built big, rectangular wooden houses up to 27 metres (90 feet) long and 6 metres (20 feet) wide. These are called *longhouses*. In each area people had different kinds of pottery. In Eastern Europe they also made many little clay figurines.

Megaliths

Some of the most interesting Neolithic monuments have been found in Northern and Western Europe. These are huge tombs, built of large stones, or *megaliths*. Several people were buried in each tomb. Often the tombs were covered with mounds of earth. Today these mounds are called *long barrows*. Some of the largest tombs have been excavated in the Boyne Valley in Ireland. Many of the stones are covered with mysterious patterns of straight and curved lines. Late in the Neolithic Period people in Britain also began to build strange ceremonial centres. These were circular areas surrounded by a ditch and an outer bank of earth, with one or more entrances. They are called *henges*. Some henges had circles of upright stones inside.

One of the finest henges is at Avebury, in Wiltshire. A long avenue, with large stones on each side, leads up to the south entrance. Avenues of standing stones are found at other ritual centres. At Carnac, in France, for example, there are nearly 3000 stones arranged in parallel rows. It has been suggested that these stones were part of a huge astronomical observatory.

Most Neolithic ceremonial centres continued to be used in the Copper and Bronze Ages. They were often made more elaborate. The huge blocks which can be seen today at Stonehenge, for example, were set up in this period. The people who built the stone circles at Stonehenge are known as the *Beaker People*. This is because they made distinctive pottery drinking vessels which

Top left: Important prehistoric sites in Europe from the beginning of the Neolithic period to AD 100, when much of Europe had become a part of the Roman empire. More archaeological sites have been excavated in Europe than in any other region of the world.

Bottom left: Stonehenge is probably the most spectacular prehistoric monument in Britain. Travellers and archaeologists have been fascinated by it since at least the 16th century, and thousands of tourists continue to visit it every year. Stonehenge was already a ceremonial centre in Neolithic times, but the huge blocks of stone which can be seen today were not set up until the Bronze Age. Building went on at Stonehenge for about 900 years.

Below: The Heuneberg hillfort in Southern Germany, one of the best excavated hillforts in Europe. It overlooks the River Danube. The Heuneberg was occupied for about 1000 years, and excavation has shown that in the Iron Age-Hallstatt period it was the home of wealthy noblemen, who were buried in barrow tombs nearby. These nobles imported high quality Greek pottery, some of which contained wine, from the Greek colony of Marseilles in southern France.

archaeologists call Beakers. Such pottery is found throughout Central and Western Europe. The Beaker People made small tools out of copper, but they had not yet discovered how to combine copper with tin to produce bronze.

Bronze-working started in Britain around 2000 BC. Many bronze objects, particularly daggers, have been found in graves. People were buried under round mounds, called *round barrows*. Late in the Bronze Age a new form of burial rite appeared in Central Europe. The dead were burnt and the ashes were placed in pottery vessels. Large cemeteries of these *funerary urns* have been excavated. They are known as *urnfields*. In this period bronze-working had become very advanced. Warriors were well-armed with spears, swords and circular shields, and they wore bronze helmets and cheek pieces. Life at home was made easier by the manufacture of bronze tools such as axes, knives and sickles for cutting grain.

A new age dawned in Europe with the discovery of how to make iron in about 900 BC. North of the Alps the earliest iron-using peoples belong to what archaeologists call the *Hallstatt Culture*. Chieftains and members of the aristocracy, including women, were sometimes buried on or with a four-wheeled funerary wagon, made of wood, with bronze and iron attachments. Long iron swords are often found in the graves. These chieftains lived in great hilltop fortresses surrounded by strong defensive walls.

The Celts

The Hallstatt Period was followed in 500 BC by the *La Tène Period*. The people of the La Tène Age are called the *Celts*. They are known not only from archaeological finds, but also from descriptions written by their southern neighbours, the Greeks and the Romans. They were said to be tall and fair, and fierce fighters. Warriors were often buried with two-wheeled chariots and horse harnesses and sometimes even with the horses themselves. Greek and Roman writers describe great migrations and invasions of Celtic peoples, who spread throughout Europe. Celtic craftsmen were very highly skilled, especially in metalwork. Many objects of gold, silver and bronze have been found, with elaborate decoration influenced by Greek and Roman styles. The Celts also imported many things from the Mediterranean, including wine transported in bronze jugs.

The main archaeological monuments of the late La Tène Period are the fortified towns or *oppida*. They often enclosed very large areas, and were well-planned, with groups of wooden buildings divided by a network of streets. The fortifications were made of timber and stone. By about AD 100, the Romans had conquered much of Celtic Europe, as far as the River Rhine and the River Danube in the east, and almost to the Scottish border in Britain. With these conquests the Prehistoric Period in Europe came to an end.

China

The Yellow River and the Wei River valleys were the first places to be colonized in Neolithic China. From about 6000 BC there were many farming settlements in this region. The earliest farmers had beautifully painted hand-made pottery. Pots were often buried with the dead. Their main crop was millet. They also kept a lot of pigs. Pork is still the most popular meat in China. By around 2500 BC the potter's wheel had been invented. The people of what archaeologists call the *Lung-Shan* culture made very fine, polished black pottery.

The Early Bronze Age civilization which followed is called the *Shang* civilization, because the rulers were members of the Shang clan who came from the central region of the Yellow River valley. They built walled cities from which they controlled the villages of the plain.

Anyang

The most important Shang site which has been excavated is at Anyang, which became the royal capital in 1400 BC. As well as ordinary houses, there were workshops where bronze, bone and pottery objects were made. There was also a ceremonial centre for the royal family, with palaces and temples. Human and animal victims were sacrificed to the gods when these royal buildings were constructed. In special pits the burials of no fewer than 852 people, 15 horses and 5 chariots, 10 oxen, 18 sheep and 35 dogs have been found.

Not far from Anyang spectacular royal tombs were discovered. The Shang kings were buried there, accompanied by sacrificed servants and horse-drawn chariots. The magnificent bronze vessels from these and other tombs show the skill of the Shang metal-workers. Bronze objects, however, were only for the rulers and aristocrats, not for the ordinary Chinese peasants. The earliest known Chinese writing comes from the Shang period. Questions to the gods and ancestor spirits were carved on bones and tortoise shells. These are called *oracle-bones*. Thousands of oracle-bones were found at Anyang and other Shang sites.

In 1100 BC the Shang state was conquered by the *Chou* people who lived to the west. Their capital was near modern Sian. The Chou rulers divided their empire into regions which they granted to the great nobles in return for military service. In 771 BC, barbarian tribesmen captured the Chou capital. A new capital was then established at Lo-yang, further east. The Chou emperors slowly lost much of their power, and many of the regional lords became rulers in their own right. The stronger regional states

Above: Excavation of the tomb of Ch'in-Shih-Huang, near the village of Xian, in Shaanxi province. Ch'in-shih-Huang became emperor of China in 246 BC at the age of 13, and died in 210 BC. Over 700,000 convicts worked on his tomb, which took 38 years to build. Part of the tomb consisted of a large vault filled with rows of life-size pottery figures of armed warriors and of horses drawing chariots. The excavation of this vault is not yet complete, but it has been estimated that a total of around 6000 figures will be found there.

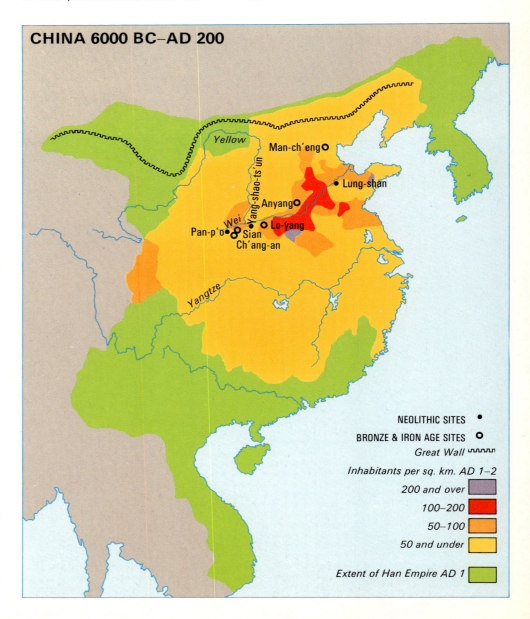

CHINA 6000 BC–AD 200

NEOLITHIC SITES •
BRONZE & IRON AGE SITES ○
Great Wall ~~~~~
Inhabitants per sq. km. AD 1–2
200 and over
100–200
50–100
50 and under
Extent of Han Empire AD 1

Above: The Great Wall of China was built by the first Ch'in emperor, Ch'in-Shih-Huang, to defend his empire against nomads – the Huns – on the northern frontier. The wall was nearly 3000 miles long. The Huns rode on horseback and fought with swords, bows and arrows. The Chinese army had both chariots and cavalry. One of their main weapons was the crossbow. Because the crossbow is very accurate at short range, it was very effective for defending the wall against the Huns.

Left: This map shows the extent of the Han empire in AD 1 and some of the main archaeological sites in China, including the Great Wall.

took over the weaker ones. During this period city states grew up in central as well as north China, as far south as the river Yangtze. Many famous scholars lived in the Chou period. One of the most well-known was the great thinker Confucius. He founded a school of philosophy which has influenced Chinese civilization to the present day.

The Iron Age in China began about 600 BC. Iron tools and weapons slowly spread throughout the land. Irrigation channels were easier to dig, and food production was increased. By 400 BC, the different regions had become independent states, which fought each other for nearly 200 years in a great power struggle. A new era began in Chinese history in 221 BC when the state of Ch'in conquered all the other states and established China's first unified empire. The empire stretched as far south as Hong Kong. The first Ch'in emperor built one of the Wonders of the World – the *Great Wall of China*.

Western people call the land China, which comes from the name Ch'in, but the Chinese call themselves 'men of Han'. The *Han* dynasty followed the Ch'in dynasty in 206 BC. It lasted until AD 220 with a break between AD 9 and 23, when a usurper briefly took control. The Han period was a glorious age in China. Chinese troops conquered

lands far into Central Asia. Through this region ran the *Silk Road*, carrying China's famous silk to the markets of the Roman empire. The first Han capital was at Ch'ang-an, near Sian, but the rulers later moved to Lo-yang, which at that time was probably the largest city in the world, with a population of over half a million people. China was already a densely populated nation. A census taken in AD 1–2 records 57,700,000 people.

Royal Tombs

The Han emperors were buried in tombs under huge artificial hills. Unfortunately none of these tombs have yet been excavated. However, two splendid tombs of a Han prince, Liu-Sheng and his wife, Tou Wan, are among the most exciting archaeological discoveries ever made in China. The burials were made in caves cut deep into the hills near Man-ch'eng in the region of modern Peking. Many beautiful things including bronzes, Chinese lacquer-work and pottery were found in the tombs. But it is the jade suits in which Liu-Sheng and Tou Wan were buried which has made these tombs famous throughout the world. Each was made from thousands of pieces of jade, sewn together with gold thread. Such things show us something of the splendour of this first great age of Imperial China.

The Romans

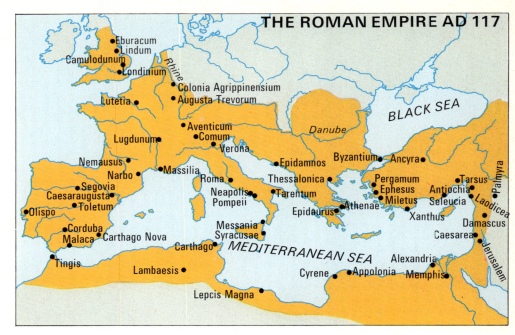

THE ROMAN EMPIRE AD 117

Before the rise of Rome, central Italy was inhabited by the *Etruscans*. The origin of the Etruscans is one of the mysteries of the ancient world. Etruscan culture seems to have developed from the previous pre-historic period in central Italy. However, most Greek and Roman writers say that the Etruscans came from Lydia in Asia Minor (modern Turkey). The Etruscans wrote in a script based on the Greek alphabet. Most of the inscriptions are either funeral epitaphs or dedications to a god. They are very short and many are still not completely understood. No other Italian languages are related to Etruscan, but a language similar to Etruscan was spoken on the Greek island of Lemnos in 500 BC. This gives some support to the idea that the Etruscans came from the East, but the problem of their exact origins remains unsolved.

They were certainly in Italy from 700 BC onwards, and many Etruscan remains, particularly tombs, have been excavated. Rich grave goods have been found in these tombs. Often the walls were decorated with colourful paintings.

At the site of Tarquinia over 150 painted tombs have been discovered. Tarquinia was just one of many Etruscan cities. Each city was independent, and had its own artistic styles and customs. The cities grew wealthy from trade with the Greek world and other areas of the Mediterranean.

In 616 BC Etruscans from Tarquinia conquered Rome, which at that time was just one of a number of villages in an area inhabited by *Latin* tribes. The Etruscan

kings transformed Rome from a village into a city. New houses were constructed and splendid temples and shrines were built.

The Roman Republic

In 509 BC the Romans drove the last Etruscan king, Tarquin the Proud, out of their city. They then established a *Republic*. There followed a series of wars with the *Carthaginians*, who had an empire in North Africa and South-west Europe. After a long struggle the Romans destroyed the city of Carthage, which was in the north of modern Tunisia, in 146 BC. These wars left them in control of the whole of Italy including Sicily, parts of North Africa, much of Spain and the islands of Sardinia and Corsica. They also occupied Greece.

Much of what we know about Roman history comes from the writings of the ancient Romans themselves. However,

Above: The extent of the Roman empire in AD 117, under the emperor Hadrian. Hadrian built a frontier wall of stone and turf in Northern England to divide the Romans from the Barbarians. During his reign a timber wall was also constructed in Germany across some of the countryside between the River Rhine and the River Danube.

Below: A street in the Roman town of Pompeii, south of Naples, which was buried under ash and lava when the nearby volcano, Vesuvius, erupted in AD 79. Archaeologists excavating at Pompeii found everything in a remarkable state of preservation. Because the Pompeians had to flee quickly from the sudden fury of the volcano, they left most of their possessions behind them. A baker even left his loaves in the oven, the charred remains of which can still be seen today.

archaeology can also tell us a lot about the Roman way of life and the organization of the empire. To help them control their newly-conquered lands the Romans built a very efficient road system. Long stretches of many Roman roads have been excavated. Where possible they ran in straight lines and each mile was marked by a pillar, starting with the *Golden Milestone* in the ancient *forum*, or market-place, in the centre of Rome. Roman citizens were settled in *coloniae*, or colonies, in strategically important places. The walls of a *colonia* were laid out in the form of a rectangle and the interior was divided into square blocks where houses and shops were built. These blocks were intersected by streets. In the centre was the forum, surrounded by public buildings – the law courts, council house and temples to the gods.

In the period between the fall of Carthage and AD 40 Rome had many clever generals and statesmen who, by a mixture of conquest and diplomacy, brought large areas of the known world under Roman control. Julius Caesar conquered most of Gaul (modern France) and many new Roman coloniae were set up.

The Roman Empire
Not long after Caesar's death the Republican government collapsed and his adopted son, Augustus, became the first emperor. During his long reign the empire was extended as far as the river Danube and the river Euphrates. Egypt also came under Roman rule. The provinces became strongly influenced by Roman ideas and the Roman way of life. Legions of the Roman army were

dispersed throughout the empire and many forts were built, especially in frontier areas. The towns which grew up around these forts often became wealthy commercial centres. Archaeologists have excavated many such towns. Like the coloniae, they had typical Roman public buildings, including bathhouses, theatres and temples. Roman coinage, pottery and other objects, language and dress were also adopted in the provinces.

By AD 117 the Roman empire had reached the limits of its expansion. Britain was conquered almost to the Scottish border where the emperor Hadrian built a great wall to defend his frontier. Some lands north of the Rhine and the Danube were also under Roman rule, and in the east, Roman territory included Armenia and Mesopotamia. As well as towns and cities there were large country estates in many provinces. Their owners lived in *villas*, with rooms arranged around a central court. Over 650 villa estates are known in Britain alone, and many of these have been excavated.

The centre of the empire was the splendid city of Rome itself. With the wealth which came from the provinces, many magnificent public buildings were erected. These included a huge amphitheatre, called the *Colosseum*, built by the emperor Vespasian. There were seats for 50,000 spectators and the opening was celebrated by games and contests lasting 100 days. The city was also adorned with statues and other works of art; there were fountains everywhere supplied by water brought from the hills along *aqueducts*. Never before had so much wealth been lavished on a city as on Rome at the height of her imperial splendour.

The Pont du Gard aqueduct, near Nîmes (ancient Nemausus), France, which was built in AD 14. It is the most splendid of all Roman aqueducts, and demonstrates the great engineering skill of the ancient Romans. It rises to 55 metres (180 feet) above the River Gardon. The water was carried in a channel above the three tiers of arches. The aqueduct was built to supply water to the Roman town at Nîmes.

The temple of Angkor Wat, built by the Khmer emperor Suryavarman II in the early 12th century AD. It is the largest building at Angkor, the capital of the Khmer empire. For a long time Angkor, lost in the jungle of Cambodia, was a mystery to Europeans. There were rumours of its existence, but it was not until 1860 that a Frenchman, H. Mouhot, reached the site and wrote about it. The huge complex of splendid buildings was completely overgrown by the jungle, and even today excavation is not complete.

Indian Asia

The historical period in India dates from the arrival in the Northwest of groups of people known as *Aryans*, some time after 2000 BC. After the downfall of the Indus civilization, the Aryans settled in the Punjab (the region of the five tributaries of the River Indus) and gradually moved south east into the valley of the River Ganges. They brought with them their sacred hymns called the *Vedas*, which were in an old form of *Sanskrit*, a language related to most modern European and North Indian languages. From these hymns we can learn something about early Aryan society. It was divided into four social groups. At the top were the priests, or *Brahmans*. Next came the *Kshatriyas*, or warriors. Third were the *Vish*, who often became merchants, craftsmen and farmers. Fourth were the *Shudras*, who had a very low social position. All non-Aryans in India were regarded as even lower than the

Shudras. This system of social groups developed eventually into the famous Indian *caste system*. The non-Aryans became the *outcastes*. We know from the texts that the early Aryans built their houses out of wood and bamboo, which quickly decay. Because of this they have left very little for archaeologists to dig up.

By around 600 BC, however, large cities had been established, and from this time onwards archaeology has more to tell us. These cities were the capitals of ancient states whose names and memories have come down to us in two Sanskrit poems, the *Mahabharata* and the *Ramayana*. Excavated sites include Ahicchatra, Hastinapur, Rajgir and Kausambi, which had a splendid palace partly roofed by stone vaults.

The years between 500 and 300 BC saw the growth of *Buddhism*. The founder of this religion was Gautama Shakyamuni – the Buddha (563–489 BC). The legendary Ashoka (272–232 BC), king of the first great Indian empire, became a Buddhist. The religion spread throughout his realm, which included almost the entire sub-continent of

India as well as parts of Afghanistan. The kings of this empire, called the Mauryan empire, ruled from the city of Pataliputra, near Patna. Parts of their splendid wooden palace have been excavated.

They also built stone monuments, including some of the earliest Buddhist *stupas*. Early stupas were solid circular domes surrounded by stone railings with gateways. They originally contained bone relics of the Buddha. The railings and gates were elaborately carved with figures of guardian spirits, animals and plants and scenes from the Buddha's life. Splendid early stupas can still be seen at sites such as Sanchi and Barhut. As well as stupas there were also Buddhist *cave sanctuaries*. At Ajanta, in West India, 27 caves were cut into the outer face of a curved gorge above a river. They date from the Mauryan period to about AD 600 and are beautifully decorated with sculptures and paintings. Ajanta was a monastery which at one time could house about 600 Buddhist monks.

The Hindus

The earliest surviving *Hindu* temples in India date from the Gupta empire (AD 320–535). *Hinduism* developed out of a combination of the Vedic religion of the early Aryans and the popular local cults of India. It is the major religion in India today. The Hindus worship many different gods. Hindu myths and legends were performed in dance-dramas in temples and at the royal courts. Many temples had special dance pavilions. Different types of Hindu temple were built throughout India by kings and members of their families.

Between AD 950 and 1150, the Chandella kings built 80 temples in their capital city of Khajuraho. Thirty of these are still standing today. Like all Hindu temples they are elaborately carved with mythical scenes and figures of the gods. Most temples have a pyramidal tower above the central shrine. This tower represents a heavenly mountain peak. As well as temples, the Hindus also built cave sanctuaries. Two of the most famous cave sites are Elephanta island, near Bombay, and Ellora in Western India.

South East Asia

When Indian traders began to set up colonies in South East Asia in the 1st century AD, Buddhism travelled with them. It became the main state religion of many South East Asian kingdoms. Much of South East Asia is still Buddhist today. One of the world's most spectacular monuments is Borobudur, a great Buddhist stupa complex in central Java, built about AD 800. Eight terraces diminishing in size and covered with elaborate carvings lead up to the central stupa. By about AD 1000 Borobudur had become overgrown and neglected, but it has now been excavated and restored by archaeologists and conservators. Many Buddhist monuments were also built in Sumatra, Thailand, Burma, Cambodia and Vietnam.

Hinduism also came to South East Asia, when Brahman families established themselves in the Indian trading colonies. It flourished in three main regions – Java, Cambodia and south Vietnam. The greatest flowering of Hindu art in South East Asia was under the *Khmer emperors* in Indochina between about AD 800 and 1200. Their capital was at Angkor in southern Cambodia, where many temples were built. Huge artificial reservoirs were also constructed there. They were connected to an irrigation system which watered great areas of the plain so that rice could be cultivated. Today in South East Asia Hinduism only survives on the small island of Bali, which has many temples and shrines, where colourful Hindu dance-dramas and other ceremonies are performed.

Above: The Kailāsanāth temple at Ellora, in central India, is dedicated to the Hindu god Śiva. It was built in the 8th century AD and was carved straight out of the solid rock of the hillside. The temple represents the sacred mountain Kailāsa, on the summit of which is the eternal home of Śiva. There are many beautiful carvings of animals and scenes from Hindu mythology all around the temple walls.

Below: Map of India and South East Asia. South East Asia was strongly influenced by Indian civilization. Indian traders set up colonies in the coastal areas. The two greatest Indian religions, Hinduism and Buddhism, travelled with the colonists, and then spread among the native South East Asian peoples.

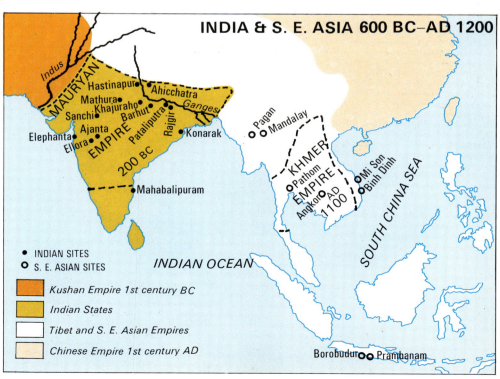

INDIA & S. E. ASIA 600 BC–AD 1200

- ● INDIAN SITES
- ○ S. E. ASIAN SITES
- Kushan Empire 1st century BC
- Indian States
- Tibet and S. E. Asian Empires
- Chinese Empire 1st century AD

Doug Post.

The Americas

Part of the central precinct of the Toltec-Maya capital of Chichén Itzá. In the background is the pyramid temple of Kukulcán, the feathered serpent. In the foreground is the great ball court where the sacred ball game is being played. The benches at the bottom have carved reliefs on them showing the two teams, Toltec and Maya. The leader of the losing team is represented having his head cut off by the leader of the winning one. The Ball Game is played between two teams who try to propel a rubber ball through their opponent's ring, using only their knees, hips and elbows. If they can put it through the ring, they win the game outright. As you can imagine this did not happen very often, but when it did, the winning team had the right to take all the clothes of the spectators.

The early history of *Mesoamerica*, that is, Middle America, is usually divided into three periods: the *Formative era* (2500 BC–AD 300), the *Classic period* (AD 300–900) and the *post-Classic* (AD 900–1520). Our knowledge of ancient Meso-america comes mainly from archaeological excavation. Several of the early civilizations had a writing system, but often the inscriptions which are preserved only tell us about a few special aspects of life and society.

During the Formative era, settled farming communities developed – agriculture became the basis of life. The main crops grown were maize, beans and squash.

Squash are plants with large fruits that look rather like melons. In part of the tropical plain along the coast of the Gulf of Mexico there lived a people called the *Olmecs*. The Olmecs were the first Mesoamerican people to use large blocks of stone for building. They built ceremonial centres with plat-forms, courtyards, altars and artificial lakes. They also carved large, stone sculptures, including strange, colossal heads. The three main Olmec centres are San Lorenzo, La Venta and Tres Zapotes.

During the Classic period, the *Maya* civilization developed in the Yucatan penin-sula and the highlands of Guatemala and Honduras. The Maya built many ceremonial centres, where platforms and stepped pyra-mids with small temples on top were ar-ranged round open courts. Each large centre also had a ball-court shaped like the letter I, where ritual ball games were played. Maya craftsmen were highly skilled. Many beautiful jade objects and carved stone stele have been found. The walls of buildings were decorated with colourful paintings and reliefs modelled in plaster. The best pottery was painted with miniature scenes of gods, priests, merchants and nobles engaged in various ceremonial activities.

The Maya had a hieroglyphic writing system. They carved inscriptions in stone and also wrote on strips of bark cloth. They had the most advanced mathematical and astronomical systems of any other ancient American peoples and they had a very complicated calendar, with 365 days like our own. The Maya were very concerned with time. They thought that different gods ruled different periods of time. Not long before AD 900, the Classic Maya civilization collapsed. We do not know why this happened. All the main sites were abandoned. Many stayed overgrown by the jungle until they were rediscovered by modern archaeologists.

In the post-Classic period, the *Toltec* state grew up in central Mexico, with its capital at Tula. The Toltecs were a warrior nation, and there are many statues and carvings of warriors at Tula. Either Toltecs or people who had been strongly influenced by them invaded the Maya region of Yucatan around AD 1000. A new civilization grew up there, which was a mixture of Maya and Toltec features. The first political centre was at Chichén Itzá, where there were many temples and other buildings in Toltec-Maya style. There was also a very large, sacred well at Chichén Itzá, into which offerings and human victims were thrown.

The last great Mesoamerican civilization was the *Aztec* civilization, which started some time after the destruction of the Toltec capital in 1170. The Aztec capital of Tenochtitlan, now Mexico City, was built on an island in Lake Texcoco. At the centre of the city was a walled precinct, within which were the temples of various gods, including Huitzilopochtli, the sun god. To help him on his daily struggle through darkness and night, Huitzilopochtli demanded hearts and blood. The Aztecs sacrificed between 10,000 and 50,000 human victims to their god each year, mostly war captives, but also slaves and children bought from their parents. The Aztecs were ruled by a priest-king, who lived in a palace near the sacred precinct. Like the Maya, they had a hieroglyphic writing system. When the Spaniards landed in Mexico in 1519, the Aztec empire was at the height of its splendour. Just two years later its power was broken and Tenochtitlan lay in ruins.

South America

While the Aztecs were ruling in Mexico, the *Inca* empire was flourishing in Peru. It rose on the foundation of earlier Peruvian civilizations, and eventually covered an area 2000 miles long and 200 miles wide. The Inca

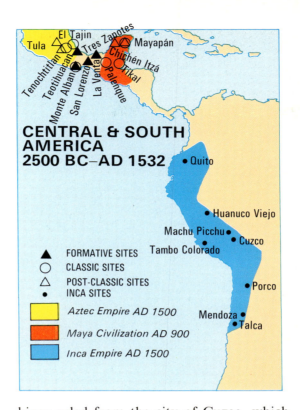

CENTRAL & SOUTH AMERICA 2500 BC–AD 1532

▲ FORMATIVE SITES
○ CLASSIC SITES
△ POST-CLASSIC SITES
• INCA SITES

Aztec Empire AD 1500
Maya Civilization AD 900
Inca Empire AD 1500

Central and South America, showing major civilizations and important archaeological sites. The American civilizations developed quite independently from the rest of the world. The Aztec and Inca empires were flourishing when the Spaniards arrived in the 16th century.

kings ruled from the city of Cuzco, which was only inhabited by the royal court and the priests. The king was thought to be the son of Inti, the sun, the main god of the Incas. The Incas were great engineers. More than 10,000 miles of road ran throughout the empire, linking Cuzco to every province. Because there were no wheeled vehicles, messages were taken along these roads by runners, and goods were transported by men or llamas. All the provinces had to provide the state with tribute, men for the army and people to work on state land. The Incas drew up many land improvement schemes, including irrigation projects and terracing of land for farming in mountain regions. But in spite of their high civilization, the Incas had no form of writing. In 1532, when the empire was at the height of its power, the Spaniards arrived. Ten years later they had practically destroyed the Inca civilization.

The best preserved Inca city left to us is Machu Picchu, built on a narrow strip of rock between two mountains, with steep drops on either side, about 2750 metres (9000 feet) above sea level. Machu Picchu is often called 'the lost city of the Incas', because after the Spanish conquest it was completely forgotten until it was rediscovered in 1911 by the American explorer, Hiram Bingham. Bingham excavated much of the city and uncovered many buildings of fine granite including the royal palace and the sun temple. He also found many burial caves outside the city, which contained the remains of 173 mummified bodies, most of them women.

Great Zimbabwe. The large circular enclosure is the palace of the ruler, with groups of huts for wives and children, for sleeping, cooking and entertaining guests. The conical tower looks like a Shona farmer's granary, and is a symbol of royal wealth. Outside the circular enclosure are other enclosures which contain the dwellings of important members of the royal court. Farmers and craftsmen also lived at Great Zimbabwe, in clay huts. Their rubbish dumps remain to show that they once lived there.

Africa

During the last few centuries BC and the early centuries AD, important changes took place in *sub-Saharan Africa*, the part of Africa south of the Sahara desert. Unlike most other areas of the world, the Africans did not discover how to make things from copper and bronze before they learned the skill of ironworking. Africa, therefore, went straight from the Stone Age to the Iron Age, with no Bronze Age in between. Knowledge of ironworking may have been introduced to sub-Saharan Africa from the north. It was a very important advance, because it meant that people had efficient iron tools and

weapons for defence and hunting and for clearing and cultivating all kinds of land, whether forest, woodland or grassland, with crops and vegetables.

Early Iron Age villagers kept sheep, goats and grew various crops. They lived in huts made of rings of upright poles, set in the ground and plastered over with clay. These huts probably had thatched roofs. On all Early Iron Age sites, archaeologists have found similar kinds of pottery. The people who lived in these villages and made this pottery probably spoke an early form of the modern *Bantu* languages. Today, Bantu languages are still spoken by over 130 million people all over Africa – from West and Central Africa to South Africa almost to the Cape of Good Hope. Swahili is a Bantu language originally spoken on the east coast of Africa between the 9th and 18th centuries. Today it is spoken by millions of East Africans.

The Iron Age

The Early Iron Age ended about AD 1000. During the Late Iron Age, early kingdoms appeared in different parts of Africa. Trade was very important for these kingdoms. From West Africa, slaves, ivory and gold, which was mined in the tropical forests, were exported across the Sahara desert to North Africa, which by that time had been conquered by the Arabs. The West African kingdoms received copper and salt, which were mined in the Sahara desert, in return. Arab writers tell us of this trade. The copper was not used for tools and weapons, but to make jewellery and ornaments for the rulers and their families.

The earliest known African kingdom was Ghana, with its capital at Kumbi Saleh. The kings of Ghana were buried under huge earth mounds. There are great numbers of these mounds in the inland delta of the River Niger. Several of them have been excavated. They contained bodies covered with ornaments of copper and gold. South of Ghana was the kingdom of Mali. Its capital was probably at Niani, a site which is now being excavated. During the Mali empire, the River Niger became very important for trade. The wealthy trading cities of Timbuktu, Jenne and Gao, capital of the Songhay kingdom, grew up along the river.

Ife and Benin

In the tropical rain forest of south-west Nigeria is the site of Ife, the sacred city of the *Yoruba* people, which flourished between the 13th and 15th centuries. The houses at Ife had open courtyards paved with patterns of postherds and pebbles. Each courtyard had one or two altars which were often surrounded by offerings to the god. These offerings included nearly life-size statues, made of baked clay.

Another interesting site in Nigeria is Igbo Ukwu, which dates to the 9th century. Here, archaeologists have found great numbers of beautiful bronze objects in shrines and graves. One burial was very impressive. The body was dressed in a crown, breastplate, bracelets and anklets of bronze, and in one hand he held a bronze staff. He was seated on a stool, and on a mat beside him were ivory tusks and a bronze leopard skull. The body was decorated with more than 100,000 glass beads.

Between Ife and Igbo Ukwu lies Benin, the capital of the *Edo* people. The kingdom of Benin was founded in the 14th century. Many spectacular bronze and brass sculptures were found in the royal palace at Benin. The palace was surrounded by a massive earth rampart and ditch, over 15 metres (50 feet) from top to bottom.

In the 9th century, Arab traders began to establish settlements in East Africa, and by the mid-14th century there were flourishing towns on almost every island and along the coast from Somalia to Mozambique. The Arabs married the native peoples, and the culture became a mixture of Islamic and African. The religion, for example, was Islamic, but the people spoke a Bantu language, *Swahili*. The merchants exported gold and ivory to India and Arabia.

This gold and ivory came from the East African interior, where great changes took place at the end of the early Iron Age. Cattle became very important for the first time. They represented wealth and prestige for their owners. Large settlements were built, often on fortified hilltops.

Great Zimbabwe

By the 12th and 13th centuries early states had developed. One of the most impressive sites in East Africa is Great Zimbabwe,

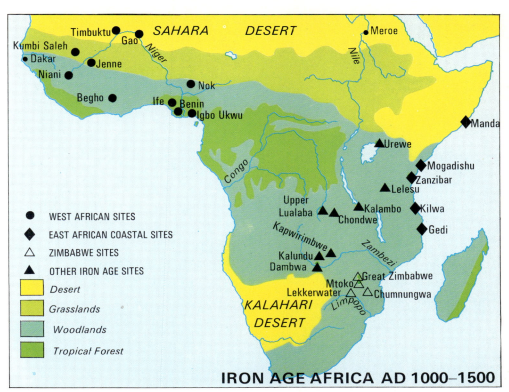

IRON AGE AFRICA AD 1000–1500

which was the capital of a *Shona* state. Shona is one of the Bantu languages. The Shona word *zimbabwe* means 'honoured house', the dwelling of a chief.

Archaeologists have excavated a circular building at Great Zimbabwe, with walls 9 metres (30 feet) high, which probably contained the palace of the ruler. Other dry stone walls have been uncovered which originally surrounded circular clay huts, probably the dwellings of the king's relatives and important high officials. Many other such stone-walled enclosures, or *zimbabwes*, have been found all over the plateau between the Zambezi and Limpopo rivers and down to the sea.

Above: Map of sub-Saharan Africa showing different vegetation zones and Iron Age sites. Iron ores were widespread in Africa. Most tropical soils contain lumps of iron oxide from which the iron can be extracted and used by the metal-workers.

Below: Groups of thatched huts in a Tuareg village near Agadez, Niger. This type of traditional African architecture has not changed very much since the Early Iron Age. Just as in the past, such villages are the home of nomadic pastoralists or peasant farmers who keep animals and cultivate various crops.

AFRICAN ART

The craftsmen of Iron Age Africa produced some very beautiful works of art. Some of the best pieces come from Benin, where a great hoard of bronze and brass sculptures was looted from the palace in 1897. At Benin the metalsmiths worked almost entirely for the Oba, or ruler. This is a bronze head of one of the Benin Obas, from what archaeologists call the 'Middle Period', that is, the 17th century AD. The Oba is wearing a collar and headdress of coral beads. The present Oba of Benin still erects altars to his royal ancestors on which many such bronze sculptures are placed.

Chronological

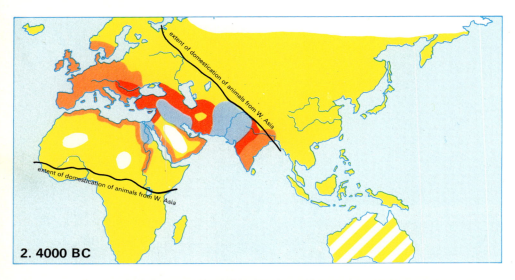

1. ORIGINS OF MAN

1. The development of the human race The shaded areas indicate how far humans had reached by the date shown. So 3 million years ago, only Homo habilis existed and it was confined to the eastern part of Africa. On the other hand, by the time North Africa, Greenland and north west Europe had been populated, people, who were the same physical shape as those today, had evolved.

2. 4000 BC

2. 4000 BC The areas of densest population are near to the great river systems. With the exception of Western Europe, most of the rest of Eurasia was sparsely inhabited by nomads and hunter gatherers. Australia was first colonized between 30,000 and 50,000 years ago, but 6,000 years ago it was still only very sparsely populated, and by nomads. Northern Russia and most of Saudi Arabia was uninhabited.

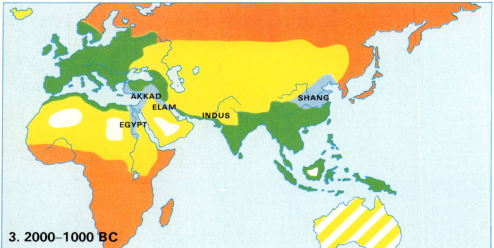

3. 2000–1000 BC

3. 2000–1000 BC By this time most of Eurasia was populated, even northern Russia. Civilizations in China, Mesopotamia and north west India were flourishing. Australia remained primitive until the 18th century. The Sahara region was beginning to dry out and the herding traditions of the central Asian plains were starting to be established.

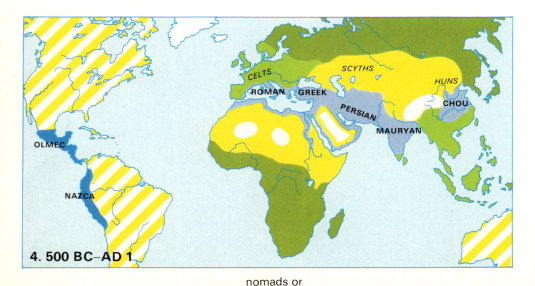

4. 500 BC–AD 1

4. 500 BC–AD 1 By now the early American states had begun to flourish. Although most of the rest of America remained sparsely populated with hunter gatherers, the Amazon area and south west of what is now the U.S.A. was Neolithic and remained so until AD 1500.

42   *Key for maps 2–8*   nomads or hunting/gathering groups   permanently-settled farming groups   Copper Age settlements   Bronze Age settlements

Atlas

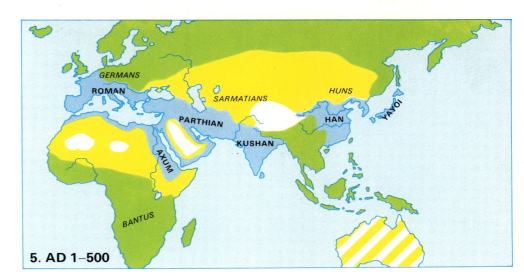

5. AD 1–500 By now the Roman empire was reaching its climax. Civilizations in Asia were flourishing. Most of the rest of Eurasia excluding the Sahara and central Asia had reached the Iron Age. In Africa the Bantu were migrating south, taking with them their knowledge of agriculture and metal working. Then gradually over this period, the great civilizations declined.

6. AD 500 At this point there is a gap between the collapse of the great civilizations and the advent of the barbarian nomads as a power. Northern Russia is beginning to depopulate as the people move south. Asian crops and technology are diffused to southern Spain and North Africa.

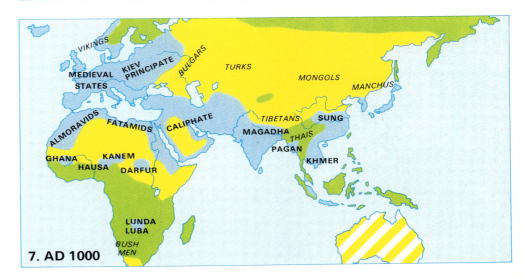

7. AD 1000 The great nomad civilizations roamed the central Asian plains wreaking havoc, driving the people south. Europe, North Africa and central Asia were now becoming quite densely populated; a city the size of London, for instance, contained over 10,000 people. The Chinese and Indian culture and technology penetrated South East Asia through trading.

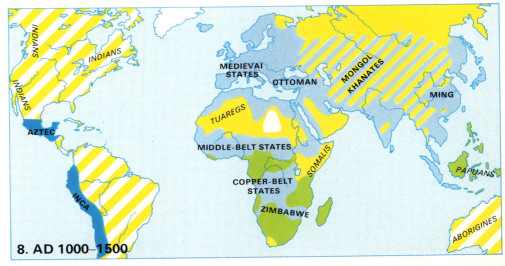

8. AD 1000–1500 In the 1200s, Mongols ruled over a great empire. Peace was established which allowed extensive trade between the east and the west. Europe derived great benefit from this. But by the 15th century, the Mongol empire had fallen, law and order had broken down, and with it the great trade routes deteriorated, because of the presence of bandits. This caused a tremendous setback in Asian civilization. Meanwhile West Africa was prospering. From 1500 onwards Europe also prospered and Britain was established as a major European power.

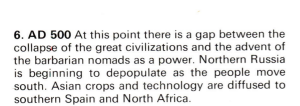

Early Iron Age settlements   Late Iron Age settlements   American states and empires   areas of dense population   INCA major civilizations

43

Index

Restoration of the Roman Orpheus mosaic at Littlecote Park Villa, Wiltshire. The Orpheus mosaic was first discovered in 1730, by William George, the steward of Littlecote House. Its location was later forgotten, and it was thought to be destroyed. Fortunately Mrs. George had made a fine embroidery of the mosaic from her husband's drawings, so historians and archaeologists knew what it had once looked like. In 1978 the mosaic was rediscovered by an archaeological team. Forty per cent of the design has survived.

ACKNOWLEDGEMENTS

Cover: William MacQuitty; Endpapers: Sonia Halliday; Title: Peter Clayton; Pages 6: top Zefa, bottom Ronald Sheridan; 7: left Zefa, right Peter Clayton; 8: Sonia Halliday; 9: top British Museum, bottom Peter Clayton; 10: top Zefa; 11: top and bottom Zefa; 12: Oxford University Research Laboratory for Archaeology; 13: top Dr. Bridgewater, top right Senate House Library, bottom William MacQuitty; 14: Michael Holford; 16: Sonia Halliday; 18: D. W. Rollin; 19: Peter Clayton; 21: William MacQuitty; 23: Peter Clayton; 24: Peter Clayton; 26: Zefa; 29: left Zefa, right Sonia Halliday; 30: Michael Holford; 32: SACU; 37: Zefa; 39: Sonia Halliday; 41: left Michael Holford, right Ian Griffiths; 44: Peter Clayton; 45: Ronald Sheridan; Back cover: Zefa.

Picture Research: Penny Warn.

Winged monster on a glazed brick frieze from a royal palace at Susa. Susa was one of the main administrative centres of the Persian empire. Darius I and Artaxerxes II both built monumental palaces at Susa. An inscription describing the construction of palaces there by Darius tells us that he used a lot of foreign materials and craftsmen.

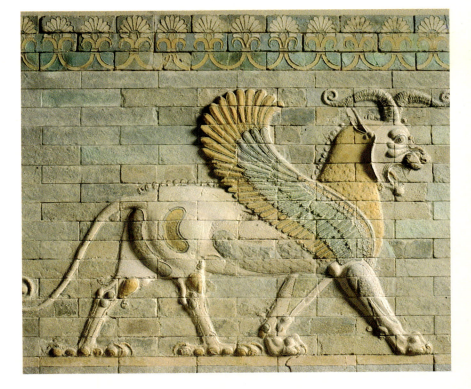